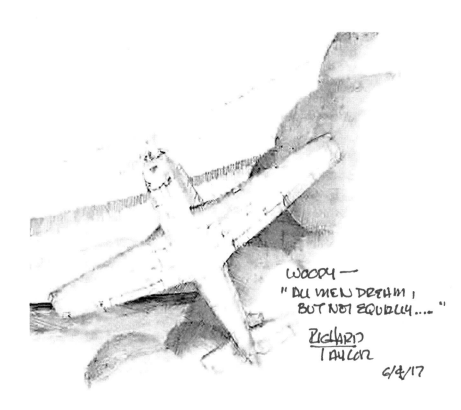

Woody —
" ALL MEN DREAM,
BUT NOT EQUALLY.... "
Richard
Taylor
6/4/17

ROLL THE POLE

RICHARD L. TAYLOR, JR.

Covers, diagrams, and sketches by the author

Roll The Pole

ISBN   978-0-9987528-0-8 (paperback)
       978-0-9987528-1-5 (hardcover)
       978-0-9987528-2-2 (eBook)

Library of Congress Control Number: 2017934798

Published by:
Full Quark Press
Atlanta, GA

"All men dream, but not equally. Those who dream by night in the dusty recesses of their minds, wake in the day to find that it was vanity: but the dreamers of the day are dangerous men, for they may act on their dreams with open eyes, to make them possible."

T. E. Lawrence (Lawrence of Arabia)
The Seven Pillars of Wisdom

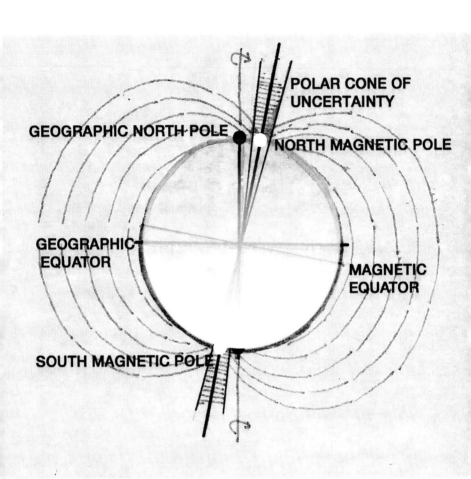

TRUE (GEOGRAPHIC) NORTH VERSUS MAGNETIC NORTH

A Geophysics 101, Refresher Course

Envision Wilt Chamberlain smiling at you while spinning a basketball on his forefinger. Assume this finger is on the Geographic South Pole. As you all know, our precious little blue planet spins like this around what's called its geographic axis. We make one revolution every 24 hours.

The ***Geographic*** Poles are the fixed locations where this invisible geographic axis intersects the Earth's surface on its top and bottom. These polar areas never directly face the sun, so they stay colder than the rest of the planet.

The *Magnetic* Poles, on the other hand, are the result of the magnetism of the molten, ferrous core deep beneath Earth's cooled and hardened shell. The soft liquefied core moves sluggishly, but independently, inside its spherical container. Occasionally the magnetic poles (the ones our compasses point to) become more or less coincident with the Geographic Poles. But it seems to be largely by chance. The geographic poles don't change location. Ask Wilt. The magnetic poles wander all the time. Ask any Arctic pilot.

According to the British Geological Survey, on average, the ***Magnetic*** Poles completely reverse their positions—north moves south and south moves north—about every 250,000 years. This reversal is called a Chron.

From the beginning of the formation of the Earth, the magnetic poles have been free to roam around at will. However, since the magnetic compass was first used only some 5,000 years ago, the Magnetic North Pole has been cruising around only in the north polar region. Most of us live thousands of miles south of there, so unless we are land surveyors or navigators, we tend to ignore the disconnection between the Geographic Poles and the Magnetic Poles.

The British Geographic Survey anticipates another Chron in 1,500 to 1,600 years. In my lifetime alone, the Magnetic North Pole has moved more than 215 miles—a distance greater than the mileage between New York City and Boston.

You've got to admit that there's some interesting stuff going on all the time right beneath our feet. And, until you play with it, you can't even feel it.

CONTENTS

CHAPTER ONE

THE FIRST GO AT THE POLE

August 1, 1978

WE ARE UP here in Canada somewhere, cruising along nicely at 7,500 feet. The weather is flawless; ceiling and visibility unlimited. And if you were up there above us looking down, and if you could peel the lid off our little airplane, you'd see Pat and me in the two front seats paying attention to things and Zip Martin spread out, snoozing in the back.

Pat Epps is flying "Left Seat." That's pilot-speak for pilot-in-command. In street-speak, it means he's driving. Right now, he's all laid back and relaxed. His fingers are barely touching the controls. In silky-smooth weather like this, and with the elevator trimmed to within a gnat's-ass of perfection, Pat lets the plane fly itself. Occasional fingertip pressure on the control wheel is only to remind the airplane spirits of the desired heading or altitude. He calls this letting the horse have its head. The horse, in this case, does not eat hay; it sucks avgas. It's a handsome, buff colored, 285 horse-power, Beechcraft Bonanza; a single engine,

1

six-place aircraft that belongs to the sleeper in the back. He flew the last leg so he goes to the end of the line.

As right seat warmer, except for emergencies, co-pilot responsibilities center on reading check lists, navigation duties, housekeeping chores and steering the airplane if Left Seat wants to take a nap. Currently, I'm folding up the aeronautical charts we used to get out of the lower Forty-Eight, and unfolding roadmaps and Canada charts for the route ahead. Other than being the librarian, housekeeping chores include policing up used paper cups, cracker wrappers, ballpoint pens and dropped napkins. We're not doing checklists. The plane is too familiar. The way we handle that task in a little plane like this is to let the pilot run through the procedure however he wants, and then, at his peril, the copilot can criticize according to mood.

As you might expect, navigation in the States is a model of electronic exactitude. And, like learning anything procedural, once you get the hang of things, it's second nature. You always know where you are and where you're going. Well, nearly always. But if you don't know, or you daydream too much, you're on Big Brother's radar screen. Should your altitude or heading wander a little bit, you'll get a polite query from an air traffic controller verifying your altitude or destination. "November 1928 Yankee, say your heading."

For this trip we're on now, we've left that more sophisticated system behind us. We are navigating by magnetic compass only. It's an imperfect science that requires more than a little hands-on experience. I'm sure that Canadian or Alaskan bush pilots might look upon our uneasiness with a knowing grin, but that's the price we pay to join their club. Eating crow is a time-honored practice not limited to pilot cults.

I think of navigating with a mag-compass as like finding the bathroom in an unfamiliar hotel suite in the middle of the night with the lights off. You know you gotta go. You know the general location of where it is and you finally get there. But direct and precise, it ain't.

Our next stop is Churchill, Manitoba. My task is to give Pat the compass headings that will bring their airport right up under the big spinner on the Bonanza's nose. Between Pat's job and mine, I have the better one. I get to think. Pat's pretending he's an autopilot. Actually, the plane does have a real autopilot, but it doesn't work. While taxing across a pasture in Mexico a couple of years ago, Zip ran it into a ditch, crumpled the landing gear and bent a wing spar. It all got looked at, and most of it got fixed. Apparently, there are still a few items left on the punch list.

Churchill lies several hundred miles ahead. Their Chamber of Commerce must take no small measure of pride in having nicknamed it "The Polar Bear Capital of the World." I guess they figure that moniker is a little more marketable than "The Frozen Capital of Nowhere." Of importance to us is that they have a jumbo airport on the shore of the Hudson Bay. It should be easy to find, and they're supposed to have plenty of gas. When we get there, we'll be about 1,650 miles from our ultimate destination: the ever-wandering Magnetic North Pole.

It's amazing how quickly the world changes at the Canadian border. The well-controlled (over-controlled?) society of the USA abruptly switches into flannel shirts and brogan boonies. Radio contact with air traffic controllers petered out an hour ago. The transponder in the panel picks up no radar blips. No one is tracking us. Except for an occasional distant AM radio station playing Country and Western music, there are no radio beacons to navigate by. The AM stations can be picked up on the plane's old fashioned direction finder, not dissimilar in use from the one Charles Lindbergh used to fly the Atlantic in 1927. Again, like Lindbergh, the lethargic magnetic compass is our sole source of navigation.

An aircraft mag-compass does not have a needle pivoting on a pin like the Boy Scouts use. In a plane, the compass looks like a short, black, heavy-walled beer can on its side with the bottom replaced with glass. Inside it you see a floating black sphere almost the diameter of the can with white directional numbers on it. The ball is magnetized to respond to the polar forces of the earth. It's mounted right there where you can't miss it, dead-center of the windshield like a round rear-view mirror. If that sounds primitive, it is.

During WWII, these things were called Whiskey Compasses. As the tale goes, crew members (or pilots) would extract the alcohol for purposes other than strict military use. Another guess on the origin of the name is that the compasses were originally known as wet compasses, and Whiskey is the military phonetic word for W. Either way, the magnetic compass is a fundamentally important back-up navigation device, but a lazy-assed primary instrument for cross-country flying. With the slightest turbulence or any changes in flight direction, or even altitude, it loses its sense of duty and wanders off on its own in search of who knows what.

Canada steadily scrolls by below us. From up here, the land is both elegant and inaudible. At altitude, looking down, the earth has a sense of loneliness to it. That image is thoughtful, but not thoughtful enough to encourage conversation with my friends encapsulated up here with me. You just feel it, and that's its own satisfaction.

Besides that, the noise level in this plane is fairly high; certainly, too high for idle chit-chat. This further isolates each of us a bit. But with two Type-A's, and easy-going-me on board, noise-dampening is probably something of a blessing.

Our airspeed is steady at 175 mph. The Bonanza's engine gauges are all stable and in the green. Both wing tanks are indicating more than half full. Everything is looking just like it's supposed to. What is the old expression? "Everything's Jake."

If you are still up there watching, surely your exceptional perception will soon catch a few things a little out of whack. At first blush, it's not obvious. You see just another little airplane flying over the Canadian wilderness, hundreds of miles off the beaten airways. But then you spot it. It is not what's there. It's what's not there. Inside the plane, you find absolutely no evidence of any survival gear whatsoever — no tents, no sleeping bags, flares or firearms. The two Type A's and the easy-going one are barreling due north, and there is not the first hint of rations, gloves, hats or cold weather clothing — not even an old aviator's leather jacket. You spot only three small gym bags with probably one change of underwear and on the floor is a blue plastic cooler into which you don't bother to look. You know what sort of entertainment guys like these would carry in a cooler. This would be considered travelling light — very light — even if they were overnighting at the Daytona stock car races.

You can only wonder what they are thinking. From your perspective, you might even wonder if they are thinking at all. Your expression is probably somewhere between a smile and a frown. I can sense that your eyebrows are closely knit.

Of course, warm and snug inside the plane, the crew has no idea that anybody's watching. Scrutiny and judgment are the farthest things from their minds. Obviously, these are three free spirits on an escapade.

Your guess might be that they are lost in Target Fixation. I think that's what old fighter pilots used to call going after the enemy even though you were out of ammunition. Race car drivers call it the Red Mist — knowingly going through turns faster than they know is possible — and it comes as no surprise to them when they go spinning off the course and brace for the looming impact of the safety wall. They knew they would spin out, but they did it anyway. Perhaps it is a failing in certain kinds of mindsets. Who knows?

In the case at hand, you are simply watching emotion cloud reason. No big deal. We all do it. Even you up there. Who among you hasn't had a romance that didn't have a chance in hell, or taken some kind of personal risk that didn't work out? Not one of you, I wager. And I bet that's why you're being so patient. Am I right?

Okay, back to the little airplane in question. The Arctic-blue Canadian sky above is still unblemished, and the sun is reflecting even more light into the cabin off the right wing. Below, cumulus puffballs are scattered out to the horizon. There's almost no evidence of man's relentless trespass on the rich, forested terrain below.

At the end of the Great Ice Age, and after the melting of the glaciers in America, this great plain was left as flat as a pool table. The unscarred timberland below shows off nature's incredible healing powers. To some of us, it reinforces the notion of tangible eternity.

Dropped randomly across the landscape like wet puppy mistakes on a green shag rug are hundreds of small, irregular lakes.

Laying that failed-but-what-was-supposed-to-be-clever metaphor aside, it looks like it smells fresh and ripe down there. I try to breath in the pine spores and summer pollen, but as far as I can tell, none of it gets up this high.

You can imagine the forest-traces of mushrooms, pine needles and the nectar scents of wild flowers competing with the rot of old trees and underbrush decay. Instead, up here, we have only the familiar smell of airplane. For some reason, all planes seem to smell about the same. It's mostly e*au de Valvoline* with a hint of avgas and some faint overtones of plastic. Unlike cars, the upholstery and musky cloth smells never seem to completely go away. A few years ago, I had a chance to fly one of Delta's Boeing 747 simulators. Even it smelled like a real airplane. So maybe it's just left over pilot-scent. Maybe all pilots naturally smell like stale stuffing and burnt fuel. Who knows? Many pilots have been accused of worse.

We're looking forward to visiting Churchill. It would really be good to check out the Polar Bear thing. Apparently, they relish frolicking in the city landfill outside of town. I believe there are sightseeing trucks that take tourists out there to watch the bears. Also, I've read that there are frequently white Beluga whale sightings in the Bay. On the other hand, planning and programming doesn't seem to be one of the exceptional attributes of our little group. So far, we're more like, Ready, Fire, Aim.

Back to navigating. I just give Pat a heading to point the nose of the airplane 15 degrees to the right (south) of a direct course to Churchill. The idea of this is to build in a known error. This way, when we hit the shoreline of the Hudson Bay and if we still don't see the airport, we know to turn left. Without this known error, if we don't see the town at the shoreline, we could only guess which way to turn. It's an old seafarer technique to find distant islands.

Like the Ancient Mariner or Ferdinand Magellan, our headings are determined only by burning desire and a wandering compass. To be fair, though, we modern types still have a tremendous advantage. We have accurate clocks and speedometers that allow us to calculate distance by multiplying speed by elapsed time. The salty old sailors of yore could only dream of such luxuries. Where they measured time by days, we measure it in seconds.

Currently, our basic plan is to find Churchill, check into a hotel, maybe look for Polar Bears, but *definitely* have a great meal. Then tomorrow we'll fly north to Resolute Bay and spend the next night. The range of the plane is 900 miles, so we'll need to find somewhere between those two towns to refuel. We'll have to figure that one out when we get to Churchill. The following day, Friday, we three will fly out to the Magnetic North Pole. Now what can be more fun than that?

Information taken from our aviation charts suggests that the Magnetic North Pole currently lies at the southern edge of the Arctic Ocean, along the most northerly coastal islands of Canada. Canadians call this their Arctic Archipelago.

We plan to locate the polar site by following the mag-compass until it reverses on us. That should be the Magnetic North Pole. We will then perform our little aerobatic gesture directly above it. Then we fly back to Resolute Bay to celebrate this momentous pinnacle of unquestionable glory. Thereafter, we'll start the long but anticlimactic flight back home to family, jobs and the rest of the real world experience.

This last phase of the journey home should be a cakewalk. It's a three-day, 3,300-mile downhill descent all the way. And as we make our way south, the navigation will become easier and the pit stop opportunities more plentiful.

Obviously, you up there know something that these three pilots don't — the existence of the Cone of Uncertainty, as shown on the Geophysics 101 Refresher Course diagram in this book. They still think the Magnetic North Pole is a sharply defined point, like a navigation beacon, and not a diffuse area many miles in diameter. But we'll get to that real-life lesson in due time.

I think many would agree that flying to the Magnetic North Pole does not stir the heart of every daydreamer amongst us. But at one time or another, nearly all of us have thought about doing something just for the randomness of doing it. Or as my old Alaskan friend, Gordon Scott, would say, "Do it just for the halibut." It's classic fantasy.

But right now, for me quite honestly, this polar-notion is starting to feel a little bit over-the-top, and offering more than a little room for pause. What the viewer from aloft, you in this case, is starting to see more clearly, we three participants are only beginning to fathom.

While we have a minute, it's important to pause this narrative and clarify something. This is a true story. It is as accurate in detail as I can make it. It is based on my Pilot Log Books, my journals, my remembrances and subsequent conversations with the participants. There is only one difference in Pat Epps' and my recollections of an event described herein. It has to do with the location of a conversation. But because I am more confident of my memory than I am of his, I have used mine. The substance of the issue involved is identical in each of our minds.

The whole notion of you, the reader, looking down on these events is obvious fantasy. Please do not take any offense. This is my way to borrow a wiser pair of eyes to see what is invisible to us at the time. Your perspective is looking back in time. Our eyes are blind to the future.

Of course you were not there then, but I would like to think you are here now.

The facts described herein are the frame and structural backbone of the story. The feelings, the disappointments, the anxieties, are the nervous system of the story. And, even though the latter is subjective, I will try to be as honest with it as I am with the structure.

Sorry for the interruption. But, as I said, it is important. Now, back to the story. *That sounds like the end of a commercial break from back when we used to listen to the radio, doesn't it?*

The engine drones on faithfully, and the hours tick by methodically. But every minute that passes pushes us a little farther away from security and a little closer to the unknown.

As I mentioned earlier, little airplanes are noisy. In the absence of conversation, I sense that each of us is giving more thought to this thing that started as a folly just yesterday. This whole effort is now taking on a life of its own. My personal feeling is not regret. It's more like apprehension, and the recognition that a little planning might have gone a very long way before we got this far down the road. In case I caught you speed reading, this is an understatement of epic proportions.

To show how tenuous this trip is, we disguised our unpreparedness with a display of false confidence in the Canadian Flight Service Station at the Thunder Bay Airport some three hours ago. The purpose of stopping there was four-fold: to clear Customs, to refuel, to get a weather briefing and to file a Canadian flight plan. But the whole conversation with the briefer added a new gravity to this trip that it didn't have when we dreamed it up yesterday afternoon. Sitting under a wing at an air show with adult beverages is one thing. Long-haul flying over a featureless wilderness is something altogether different.

While Pat and I watch unchanging Canada slide steadily under the leading edge of the wing, the idea of responsibility versus adventure is bouncing around in the back of my brain. The lack of conversation between us tends to magnify the uncertainty of our decisions. It's simply too noisy in here to open an easy discussion like, 'You know, Klondike? I've been thinking about all this…"

Oops. This conversation reminds me of something I forgot to tell you. Pat Epps' airport name is Captain Klondike.

It seems that a few years ago he flew a little tail-dragging Cessna from Atlanta to somewhere in Alaska. That's a long trip by any standard, but the real hook was that the airplane didn't have any radios or navigation instruments. It was pure, seat-of-the-pants, puddle-jumping, bush-piloting. The Cessna, however, did have a magnetic compass. In our close-knit circles at the airport, the exalted handle, Captain Klondike, stuck.

Back to how we might have avoided this entire screwy thing.

Imagine how productive a *mano y mano* discussion might have been if we could have had one.

But, think about this. Suppose we had reasoned ourselves out of this hair-brained scheme? The answer's simple. Then it never would have happened.

But it did happen. And it turned out to be important. You'll see.

Now, mile by mile, we're being pulled into something quite compelling, and it's way beyond where we've ever been before. Yes, there is magnetism pulling us to the Magnetic North Pole. Hell, we can feel it from here. But the heading indicator floating in alcohol is not altogether steady. Nervousness is gradually becoming evident in both the magnetic compass and our own personal moral compass. And nobody has any idea what *that* direction indicator floats in.

Well, let me back up a little. I can only speak for myself on this apprehension issue. Pat and Zip might have entirely different perspectives. Remember, because of the noise, we're not sharing what's going on inside our respective heads.

I calculate we are now about 350 miles north/north-east of Thunder Bay. This puts us at about the midway point between there and Churchill. The reflections of a hundred lakes continue to mirror the blue sky. The dark green-black shadows of the clouds below move steadily across the forest-scape. I pick points in the trees to track cloud-shadows to get an idea of wind direction. It is a quartering tailwind from the west. Thank You for small blessings.

My mind is still digesting what the Canadian Flight Service agent told us. He warned, "Gentlemen, you know that you should take the gyrocompass out of the plane before you get to the Magnetic Pole, don't you? The teams I know who work up there all do that."

This made no sense to me. Not wanting to confuse the issue, we didn't mention to him the part about flying upside down when we got there.

That conversation is only a couple of hours old. It hasn't had time to thaw.

Then, without the least warning, like someone pulled a lever-switch, the steady, sweet sounding motor erupts: **Knack! Knack! Knack! Knack!**…

I immediately reach for the throttle to pull off the power. Pat's hand is already there easing it back slowly. I tell him, "You just keep flying, Klondike. I got the engine." My hand is on top of his. He's not quick to let go. He does one more quick scan of the engine gauges before he relinquishes throttle control.

The knocking didn't start gradually. Something mechanical just broke. It sounds internal in the engine. Its cadence is like a connecting rod or a stuck valve hitting a piston. It's not terribly loud, but it sounds serious. Metal hitting metal. That can't last long.

I scan all the gauges, and I then scan them again. There are no aberrations. Every needle is centered in the green sector of the gauge. This can't be. I must be missing something. Then, because my brain is racing and my instrument scan is going everywhere too quickly, I use my finger as a guide to slow down my brain. I touch each gauge one by one, almost, but not quite talking to it. *Oil pressure gauge. You're exactly on 66 psi. Right in the middle of the green. Now stay there. I'm watching you.*

I then go to the oil temperature gauge. There must be something here to support the noise. The oil pressure is still normal; the needle doesn't waiver. The oil temp stays steady in the green. It could be a collapsed valve lifter, but the engine isn't missing a beat. It's running smoothly. A broken piston ring would cause a definite engine miss from low compression. But it wouldn't sound metal to metal. But it might smoke from blow-by. There are no vibrations. I ease back on the throttle but keep the engine at 2,400 rpms.

No change in the knocking.

Carefully, I go to full-rich fuel mixture. No change. Then to half-rich. No change. Then I lean the fuel mixture control until the engine stumbles. This doesn't change the racket. I try other combinations. With less power, the airspeed drops to 155 mph. I check everything again, and all the instrument needles still read normal. Fuel pressure hasn't wavered, so I skip the auxiliary fuel pump drill. Then, just in case the fuel pressure gauge isn't working properly, I try a little boost pump just to see if the fuel-pressure gauge responds. It does. It's spooky to not have any evidence of what's wrong.

But we're still flying. The engine is still running on all six cylinders. And still knocking. Pat is watching me like a hawk. We're not talking, but we're communicating. He knows exactly what I'm doing.

Next priority: If we're going down, we need to know where we are. I spread the aviation charts out on my lap. The visual ones have lakes, towers, and, best of all, airports depicted as colorful circles. My focus is to locate any airport and every paved or unpaved road within 50 miles. Of course, I don't know where we are, so there are none. I check the charts for roads usable for an emergency landing miles away from where we might be. I'm also looking out the window for clearings in the forests below.

There are none.

By multiplying our airspeed by time gives us an arc from Thunder Bay. Then by drawing a line of our magnetic course, it intersects that arc. That is where we are supposed to be. I cannot find enough information on the ground below to match anything on the map. I'm trying to match featureless terrain with nothing, and it ain't working.

If the engine quits, it looks like a water landing in a lake might be the best choice. There are no open fields anywhere in sight.

"Alright, Pat. Whatcha think?"

It has not been ninety seconds since the start of the engine racket.

Unruffled, Pat banks the plane to the left and calls the next shot. "We're headin' back to Thunder Bay. You check the charts for anything we can land on. And keep looking out the window, too. And keep picking clearings. I'll scan my side. You scan yours."

What the hell you think I been doing? runs through my head, but I don't say anything. I just nod and give a little hand movement. Our brains are in the exact same place.

Then he adds, raising his tone a little, "And keep your eye on the oil pressure. Also, quit fooling with the engine. Once you get it where you want it; then just leave it alone. Your messin' with it makes me nervous." He's totally expressionless — like he's deep in thought. His hand is firmly gripping the control wheel. The plane is not flying itself anymore. Not even a little bit.

This time I do answer, "Okay, man. I sure would hate for you to get nervous right now."

Of course he's right. If the engine is running well enough to keep us aloft, tinkering with it to find new boundaries is only inviting new opportunities for mischief.

The plane keeps droning on, and the engine continues knocking.

A very long two hours later, Thunder Bay finally comes up on the horizon with the magnificent expanse of Lake Superior right behind it. What a beautiful sight. We start relaxing. Pat puts us down on the long runway and taxis to the fueling apron. A lineman flags us in. Pat shuts down the motor, and, with a feeling of satisfaction, we all three finally exhale.

That was tense.

Only because we made it back can we say all the decisions were the right ones. Had we not made it, our judgment calls would be viewed very differently. But if you think about it, there were only a couple of options. One could argue that, because it was a little closer, we should have continued on to Churchill. Another second-guesser might take the position that we should have landed at the first available field, either natural or gravel strip. Pat made his calls intuitively, and I completely agreed with him. He is incredibly good at making a quick assessment of a situation and then figuring out if he has a little time to evaluate things. In aviation, many decisions don't have much of a thoughtful component to them. Time could be measured in microseconds before it's too late.

Pat, on many levels, could write the book on decision-making. He will make a few more on this trip, however, that I will be less comfortable supporting.

It ain't over yet. In fact, we're just beginning.

While the plane is being refueled on the ramp, Pat and I open all the engine inspection panels. There is no evidence of oil seepage or of anything broken. The engine is clean as a pin. We crank it up again with the brakes on and the wheels chocked, rev the engine to full power and there is neither exhaust smoke nor engine blow-by. Standing unsteadily in the prop blast even at an idle we try to hear if the rattle is coming from one of the magnetos. It's impossible to tell.

The noise has not changed. We shut the engine down again.

After tidying up his rat's nest in the back of the plane, Zip says, "It's past six o'clock. I don't think we're going to find a mechanic this late. So what's the plan? If we're hanging out here, I'm buying." He's happy, pumped up and ready to go to town.

Pat's still on his knees looking for gremlins in the belly pans. He crawls out, gets up and replies, "I didn't lose anything in Thunder Bay. Let's go on to Chicago. We'll figure it out down there."

Personally, I'm emotionally drained. We stretched our luck pretty good just to get here.

I need to slow things down. "Hey, man. We're not just talkin' the other side of the lake here. Chicago's 450 miles away. That's three hours. Also, it'll be dark in an hour, and that'll give us two hours of night flying."

I go for support. "Zip, what do you think?"

He smiles and doesn't hesitate, "Hell, I got a bottle of Chivas in the back there somewhere, and anything's okay with me. I say, let's have some fun."

I'm a little suspicious of Zip's back seat entertainment code. But, as they say, the sun is below the yardarm somewhere. And it's his airplane.

If you don't count the annoying knock, for the last couple of hours the motor has run flawlessly with all vital signs well in the normal range on every instrument.

Out-voted, I agree. "Okay, well, let's get going then. We need to get as far down the road as we can before it gets dark."

Walking to the plane, I add, "I still want the engine."

I've built several sports car motors including an air-cooled Porsche, and that makes me think I have at least some seniority in the mechanical arena. Incidentally, Dr. Ferdinand Porsche designed the original VW Beetle engine to be installed in an airplane. The technology is transferrable. We don't discuss any of this. We just do what's natural.

Once we get back to the States, navigation duties will be a snap. It's like driving Interstates all the way. Pat's got hundreds of hours in a Bonanza compared to my dozen or so. He stays Left Seat.

We'll get back to how the flight goes from bad to worse as we leave Thunder Bay in a little bit. But first let's backtrack to see how this whole North Pole thing got started just yesterday at the Oshkosh Air show in Wisconsin.

We land at Witman Regional Airport, Oshkosh, Wisconsin, at 8:45 am. The three of us spend the day on our feet gawking and marveling at all things aviation: airplanes, radios, jazzy paint jobs, gliders, fighter planes, old bombers, Piper Cubs, hang gliders and parachutists. The temperature has been in the 90's and the weather is what pilots like to call *severe clear*. By tea time, we're saturated with sun, crowds, 18-cylinder radial engines and cute honeys promoting aviation insurance programs. We seek the solar protection of the airplane. There also happens to be a blue plastic cooler in it that fits under a wing nicely. Stretching out in the shade before dinner with a cold beverage in hand feels pretty good.

Sitting under the wing of a low-wing airplane is a lot like hiding under someone's old front porch. Except for spider webs, it's all about headroom. The need for shade and rehydration eclipses even the sonic lure of distant aerobatic aircraft demonstrations. Protected from the sun, our little haven at the airport becomes an unintended incubator for random thoughts and plotting the ridiculous. Although it is not as easy as it used to be, nose-to-the-grindstone, working class adult men can still do it. Just watch.

The sprawling acres of freshly mowed grass between the runways are crisp and green and smell of summer. For added spice, there's a dash of engine oil, a fresh sprinkling of aviation gasoline and an occasional whiff of spent Jet-A kerosene. Perfect! Off in the distance we listen to aircraft engines whining over the main runway. Supersonic propeller tips howl as an unseen plane dives straight to earth. Then deep growls sound-off as that same airplane labors vertically to recapture its lost altitude. The routine is a carefully balanced dance of momentum versus power and energy conserved versus energy arrogantly spent.

Then there's a new sound. Phomp, Phomp, Phomp. Right away, all of our ears pick it up. It's the same plane doing a series of inverted snap rolls making phomps like beating a pillow with a ping-pong paddle.

With my back against the left main landing gear, I find a little headroom in the wheel-well. Just because it's there, like right in my face, I inspect all the components of the landing gear assembly close up. Actually, the mechanism is completely unpretentious, almost primitive in its simplicity. There is just a big hinge at the top and a hydraulic push rod. What could be simpler?

To get some conversation going, I pose to my captive audience a question. "You know what? Here we are, three pilots hunkered under an airplane full of fuel and lots of charts. We've got plenty of imagination, some dollars in our pockets and a little time on our hands. We need to go somewhere."

Pat is stretched out under the belly of the plane. He looks to be catnapping, but I think it's only a ruse.

Almost without hesitation, keeping his eyes closed, he grunts "Lez go to Narsarsuaq."

Narsarsuaq is a helluva arbitrary suggestion. I know it only by reputation. It's a small settlement on the southern tip of Greenland. During WWII, it was known as Bluie West One and served as a fueling stop for planes coming and going to Europe. It's still in operation as a major way-station for military and civilian aircraft making the trans-Atlantic haul. I like the idea only because it's totally crazy. But, to me at least, it doesn't carry enough *weight of destination.* It's not relevant to anything we're doing here. Trying to come up with something even more off-the-wall, I shuffle the charts.

"Naw, what we need to do is to go to the North Pole."

Zip looks over at us, "What the hell you guys talking about?"

"To the North Pole, man. Where'd you think?" I don't mention Narsarsuaq.

Zip is sitting yoga-style out by the wingtip where there's more headroom and a little breeze.

"Who the hell brought up the North Pole, anyway?" says Zip. "I thought you guys were figuring out a place to eat dinner tonight."

"Lookie here." I'm talking while I'm shuffling charts. "We've already come 750 miles from Atlanta. Then from here to the Pole is only another twenty-four hundred miles. We're almost a third of the way already."

No. Don't bother to check my math. I'm selling, not buying.

"Well, I'm still liking Narsarsuaq." Pat hasn't given up.

He starts a pitch, "Ernie Gann flew there in a DC-3. You guys ever read *Fate is the Hunter*? We need to do what Gann did. Besides we're a third of the way there already."

There is no need to check his geography either. At this point, it's all about marketing, not statistical accuracy.

Zip pulls out a Paul Masson wine carafe from the blue cooler and twists off its palm-sized cap. It's dripping cold. In a crawling-crouch to stay in the shade, he leans over to top off Pat's Dixie Cup. That's two for him. So when it's gone, Pat's done for the day. Zip refills his own cup. You can bet he's not done. I'm okay with my can of Bud.

We're sitting under Zip's plane, which, as I said, is a very nice aircraft. It's dependable, comfortable and fast. No matter how fine this airplane is, however, it is only marginal as a serious shading device.

At birth, Zip's mother named him Verner Martin. We gave him the jazzier appellation a couple of years ago when he, Pat, Mike Pickett and I ferried a Piper Aztec from Atlanta to Birmingham, England. The word ZEP (the acronym for a big chemical company) was printed on his jacket, but ZIP suited his personality better. Hence the change.

Zip owns a box manufacturing company in Atlanta. Aside from that, he is certainly the most colorful of the three of us here. He's Epps' and my senior by ten years, which puts him in his mid-50s. He's about six feet tall, and his athletic build and posture make him look like he's always about ready to leap. There is a physical dynamic in him that is always moving. But it's his face that sets him apart. There is always that not–quite-hidden smile that stays so close to the surface that it doesn't take but the smallest notion to trigger it. It's starting to blossom now.

As he gets a little more into this North Pole thing, his posture is starting to take on a little cat-prowl to it. He's starting to nod his head just the littlest bit like he's thinking about it. Zip's smile is becoming conspiratorial. It's starting to make me nervous.

Pat shares some of these smile qualities. But rather than Zip's *walk-right-in* smile, he uses a *complicity* smile. No matter if you just met him in an elevator or if you've been buddies for years, when you're with Pat, you feel that you are included in an about–to-happen action-plot involving some sort of wholesome, Boy-Scoutish mischief. His blue eyes, graying hair, and stocky build all play into the whole action image.

As mentioned earlier, Pat runs Epps Aviation at Peachtree Airport in Atlanta. They service private aviation aircraft from Piper Cubs for weekend flyers to elegant Lear Jets for wealthy corporate executives. Epps Aviation is where the "aviation in-crowd" gather, when they come to Atlanta.

It's almost like witchcraft, but damn near everyone who meets these two guys feels immediately comfortable with either one of them. In whatever manner the *friendly gene* gets dealt out, they both got double hits.

And me? I'm probably the quietest of the three, and, hence, the journal keeper. Back in the real world I'm a partner in a small firm, Taylor and Williams, Architects, in Atlanta. We do quite respectable work.

So that's us: Zip, Klondike and Super. I'll get around to my airport name a little later. It's not very interesting.

Now, back to Oshkosh and airplanes.

Somewhat impulsively this morning, the three of us flew up here to catch the air show. Once a year, Oshkosh becomes the aviation Mecca for pilots all over the world. Our plan is to spend the night and then fly back to Atlanta tomorrow. But now that I've got my two buddies attention about heading farther north, it's time to set the hook and start developing a program.

With almost no thought to the logistics of such a mission, I go back to the pitch. What's the old saying? "Sell the sizzle, not the steak."

The aviation charts show that the Magnetic North Pole is about 600 miles closer to us than the Geographic North Pole. Every one of those 600 miles is out over the Arctic Ocean. A 1,200-mile round trip is well beyond the 900-mile range of Zip's Bonanza. Fuel capacity compels us to settle for the *Magnetic* North Pole. Besides, how many people know what a magnetic compass will do when it's exactly at the Magnetic North Pole?

The answer to that question is probably known to quite a few people with Arctic experience. But what if we take this one step further? What if we roll our airplane so that it's inverted but under positive G's while flying over the Magnetic North Pole? What will that compass do then? It's a pretty sure bet that unless you've done it, you will only be guessing. So the next question is: has anyone ever Rolled the Pole before? If this has happened, it has not been recorded anywhere that I know of.

The knowing something that nobody else knows is the hook. The destination is secondary. So I lay out the case.

"The way I see it, Churchill's a fair-sized town on the Hudson Bay. It's about 1,000 miles from here. We fly that leg tomorrow and get us a nice hotel in town. Then after supper, we hitch a ride out to the city dump and watch the Polar Bears rummage through the garbage. Resolute Bay is another thousand miles. We spend the next night there." I don't mention that we have to find a fuel-stop along the way.

I go back to pitching. "According to our charts here, the Magnetic North Pole is only about 300 miles north of Resolute. So we just keep the magnetic compass on 360 and fly on out. When the compass reverses, we're there. So we then turn right around and roll that sucker, and then fly back on the same tank of gas. That makes us the first guys to 'Roll the Pole.'"

To show my confidence, I ask Zip to pass me a fresh cool one.

He pitches me a wet can and asks Pat, "Do you know what the hell he's talking about?"

"Hey, I'm just lying here minding my own business," Pat laughs as he takes a small sip from his paper cup. Apparently, he's trying to stretch it out as long as he can before we have to crawl out from under the plane and go in search of dinner.

Zip's still thinking. "Now, tell me again why in the name of hell we want to go to the North Pole?"

I think he just nibbled the bait and I've got to set the hook. But for the first time, I'm thinking if there is a Doubting Thomas amongst us, it's starting to be me. I haven't a clue what it takes to fly to the North Pole, magnetic or otherwise. Now I'm put in a position to justify a random, impulsive and maybe irresponsible suggestion. Practical or not, there's no turning back now. We are just guys, you know. And once you start struttin'…

Rather than answering Zip directly, I turn to Pat. Maybe I can land them both this way.

"Klondike?"

"Yo."

"You were a Boy Scout, weren't you?"

"Yo."

"You had a hand compass didn't you?"

"Yeah."

"You ever wonder where it pointed?"

"No. I knew where it pointed. It pointed north."

"No, man. That's the direction it pointed. Did you ever want to know exactly where the Magnetic North Pole is on the face of the Earth, and what that place looked like?

"I don't know. Maybe."

"Okay, then didn't you always want to go there?"

Pat thought a moment about this, "No, not really. But if you want to go there, I'm game. But after that, I'm coming back through Narsarsuaq."

He bit! Well, sort of bit. Pat is seldom easy to read, but right now you can see his imagination starting to arc. He sees the North Pole thing as a concession to get to where he really wants to go, which is Narsarsuaq. We'll get to the *why* of that story in a minute.

He goes on. "You know, every airplane I ever heard of's got a magnetic compass; the Spirit of St. Louis, the F-15 fighter and even the U-2. I bet the Russian MIG-23's got one too. Yeah, we need to check this Pole thing out."

He then adds again, "But I tell you right now, one more time, we're coming back through Narsarsuaq." You know that he's not just going to cave in on this.

This is crazy. I look over to Zip. Maybe he'll bring the conversation back to reality.

"You game?"

He's smiling, "Sure, why not? Now where are we goin' to go eat dinner tonight?"

After the last air show routine, we thumb a ride to town. Just to make Zip happy, we have juicy steaks at a tablecloth-restaurant and stay at a three-to-a-room, chain motel in the middle of

Oshkosh. I get the rollaway. Because he harped so much about eating, we stick Zip with the dinner tab.

Before turning in, I call home. In fact, each one of us does. I think we all use the same flimsy excuse for an extension of time. Something like, "Tomorrow we're flying up to Canada to look around. We might need a couple of more days." To our credit the idea of going all the way to the North Magnetic Pole still seems a little beyond reason. I don't mention it, and a dollar to a donut says that the other guys don't either.

I have no apprehensions about calling Nancy. We've been married five years, and that's after palling around for nine. Most of my un-programmed impulses have been sorted out by now, and she accepts what's left of them as normal behavior. When she and I first met, my sport was professional motorcycle racing. That set the derring-do bar so high that almost anything I do now is in the normal range. But the same holds true for her, too.

She's also a pilot. Diversions of riskier pursuits have always been part of our deal together. It's a relationship different from most, but it's one that is both respectful and enduring. On top of that, she is a tall, exceptionally beautiful brunette with flashing brown eyes. When I'm caught up in some kind of nonsense — like what's going on right now — her trust makes it very easy to call home.

Eight o'clock the next morning we're in the air and on our way. This is my turn to drive, so I'm Left Seat. At the end of 300 miles of crystal blue sky, we come up on Thunder Bay, Ontario, land and clear customs. After topping off the bird, checking the weather, wolfing down a vending machine sandwich and filing a flight plan, we head north to Churchill. This is Pat's leg; I'm right seat. Zip's catnapping in the back with his best friend, the blue cooler.

When we're finally on course at 7,500 feet and things settle down, I rethink the conversation with that Canadian Aviation official that I mentioned earlier. He wasn't in a uniform, but he was still a little officious. When told that our ultimate destination was the Magnetic North Pole, his first response was cautious skepticism. He eventually came around a little, but with warnings of the Pole's effects on navigation instruments, particularly the gyrocompass. As I said, he recommended that we do what real Arctic pilots do: remove this instrument at Resolute and then reinstall it on the way back south. The assurance in his tone of voice made us think that he might know what he was talking about.

Obviously, our Polar experience is nil, and his admonition is worrisome. But nonetheless, we're on an adventure. We take off, climb back up to cruise altitude, and press on.

It is an hour and a half later that the motor starts knocking. We turn back to Thunder Bay, land, and decide to press on to Chicago.

The sun is setting on the northwest horizon when we lift off from Thunder Bay and head south. Normal take-off power in most aircraft is with full throttle. This time, however, I set the engine to the gentle cruise settings we worked out earlier. This limits the throttle to about 65 percent power. It takes a while to ease up to 7,500 feet. Even after the sun sets, the visibility is still 20 miles. We cross Lake Superior and fly down along the western coast of Lake Michigan. Our course is a mile off the shoreline, within easy gliding distance of terra firma. Even though it's after dark, we will fly visually. If the engine quits, at night, a water-landing just off-shore will probably be preferable to a night landing in the trees or on a highway.

The contrast between a zillion lights to the west and the lake's blackness is mesmerizing. The line of demarcation — the shoreline — is the brightest lit. You can't take your eyes off the scenery. Milwaukee comes up on my side, and looks like a huge pile of diamonds that's been spilled out onto smooth black velvet and then scraped with a long straight-edge to a halfway point. Scattered out on the water-side are a couple of missed sparkles.

There is no conversation going on in the airplane. What's to say? We pass by in dark silence. Not moody-dark, mind you. Just, lack of photons dark.

Thirty minutes later we pick up Chicago weather on the radio. It's almost a comic relief to hear somebody talking to us after such a long quiet spell. We need to start getting back in the game again.

The weather in Chicago is not so good, but hardly a challenge: three miles visibility with light rain. To be on the safe side, Pat radios Chicago Approach Control and requests an instrument approach into Midway Airport. Chicago Approach is efficient and accommodating. We've missed rush hour. I dig out the correct approach plate from the three-inch thick loose-leaf manual and hand it to Pat. We land right in the middle of a crowd of eight million people. In its nocturnal splendor, Chicago is simply dazzling. From our outsiders' perspective, there is no crime, strife, poverty or political controversy in this city. Instead, after a long and apprehensive flight, Chicago generously offers us a welcome safe harbor for the night.

As we taxi to the service facility, the motor is still knocking. It's 10:15 pm local, and except for the piercing glare of a few halogen lights, the airport is as dark as pitch. The runways, taxiways, and aprons are glistening wet. The entire airport is either intensely black or brilliantly reflective. Other than the blue taxiway lights, there is no color on the airfield. The overcast reflects the yellow glow from the city. Its puffiness is like a giant dark comforter we're hiding under. Actually, it feels sort of good and safe.

But, most importantly, we made it. Time for a second, deep exhale. Finally, we're ready to relax.

The fuel truck tops us off with 100 octane avgas. I pay for it at the counter and meet the boys at the plane to help unload.

Walking up to them, I catch something suspicious in the dark silhouette of Pat's body language. He's moving around in quick motions. He's still pumped. His shoulders are a little bit forward. He keeps looking around more than he needs to. And he sure as hell ain't unloading the airplane. Just like you up there, I know what's coming even before he says a word.

Over his shoulder, without eye contact, he calls, "Come on. Lez go. We're gonna keep going. I'm driving."

I'm tired. I can feel fatigue dampening my brain waves. But I can also feel an adrenalin-hype seeping in through the cracks. This is not good by any measure; it shouldn't be happening. But for some reason, leaving fatigue aside, our continuing on to Atlanta seems like the next logical step.

Logical step? Come on. If anything, we're looking at corrupted logic. We woke up this morning with high spirits to fly to the Magnetic North Pole. Here we are now, 1,500 miles later, headed home with our tail between our legs, into a midnight flight with a knocking engine. *Corrupted logic* is far too generous a term.

But what say Ye up there looking down? You just going to watch?

The engine certainly isn't getting any worse, and we're only 600 miles from home. In that light, pressing on may not be a totally imprudent decision; that is until we call Flight Service and get the enroute weather.

The briefer reports that lying across Kentucky is a mature cold front with a line of heavy thunderstorms running unbroken from south Alabama up through eastern Ohio. The direct course to Atlanta is blocked solid. Obviously, this is a game changer. I shouldn't need to, but I again lay out to Pat the inadvisability of continuing this flight. We're in a plane without weather radar, with an exhausted crew and an engine with an undiagnosed noise. The only thing going for us is that we have five hours of fuel for a four hour flight. Like big deal.

Pat's mind is made up, and he has no interest in discussing options, logical or otherwise.

Obviously, there is something else going on in his head that he's not sharing. I wish I could offer you the key to that shut door, but I cannot. No. Let me take that back. Even if I had it, I would not offer it, because it's Pat's door. If you want it know what's going on in his head, I'm the wrong one to ask. Ask Pat.

Zip is happy as a pig in poop in the back seat. He wants to keep going anywhere Epps wants to go. He thinks Epps can part the waters and hang the moon. On top of that, having discovered that an empty Paul Masson carafe makes a perfect pee-bottle, he's now invincible.

Pat's unwavering determination to press on prevails again.

I have to remind myself; in his *lez go* mode, Pat is a compelling leader, but he's also not immutable. He's difficult to turn around because unwavering determination is part of the natural leadership matrix. But he can be turned around. I've done it before but it's grueling work. It's something you don't want to enter into lightly.

If this decision to press on tonight turns out to be a poor one, it will probably end as a fatal event. The stakes are that high.

So why would one take such a risk? you might ask from up there.

Simple. Some see their lives as larger, more vibrant and more luminous when exposed to the radiant light of risk. Others are more comfortable when they insulate their lives with thick, protective safety-cushions. Neither is right, and neither is wrong. They're just different.

With respect to the issue at hand, just like all of the other consequences in life, each of us takes the same responsibility for supporting a decision, as others must take for initiating it. There is no difference between the two. The responsibility is divided equally. This applies to both the risk-takers and the safety-cushion huggers. And that's just the way it is.

After filing our Instrument Flight Plan to Atlanta, we half-eat cold, white bread sandwiches from the coin-fed machine, throw away the rest, and climb back in the plane. I'm still right seat. I feel as one with the motor. I don't want anyone, especially Epps, fooling with its settings.

Well, there is an exception to this. For take-off and climb-out, the pilot has to keep his right hand on the throttle. If there is an engine failure at the moment we leave the ground—at rotation—all control must be maintained by the Pilot in Command. Decision-making at this critical point in a flight is instantaneous and not even a little bit democratic. I do, however, ask Pat to use 65 percent power on take-off.

We're cleared for take-off. He obliges my request with 75 percent power. He's still gotta be Pat Epps, you know.

Once we reach a thousand feet, I tell him, "I got the engine." He's fine with that. I go back to 65 percent. I still gotta be me. The engine continues to make its normal Knack! Knack! Knack! Knack!…

Since we're on an Instrument Flight Plan, we will be in both radar and radio contact with air traffic controllers all the way home. The flight starts uneventfully. There is no conversation except for occasional controllers handing us off from one sector to another. Our eyes stay pretty much straight ahead or on the charts. Well, that's both Pat and mine. I think Zip may be studying re-runs on the inside of his eyelids.

The ride for the first hour and a half is smooth and ordinary. The peacefulness tends to make the anticipation a little eerie.

But, inevitably, as we approach the Kentucky/Tennessee line, ahead of us lies the Great Black Wall, just as Flight Service had warned. The whole horizon is varying shades of black. The sky beyond the foreground clouds flickers with reflected lightning flashes. We see the cloud masses mostly in profile.

The dark clouds on our left spread to the even darker ones on our right. Along the entire eastern horizon is a line of cumulo-nimbus formations flashing visible indigestions from within their massive bellies. A dark area in the sky will suddenly light up to reveal an internally illuminated translucent creation. Then it goes black again. Running from north to south along the spine of the Appalachians, the grumbling goes out of sight in both directions.

Pat calls Center and asks for radar weather advisories. They offer no passages through the front. It's past midnight, and not much radio chatter is going on. The commercial airliners have all gone wherever they were supposed to go. Our choices are simple. We either penetrate the line or go back to the last open airport behind us, Louisville, Kentucky.

Trying to nurture any little bit of help from FAA, Pat calls Center again. Sometimes even he isn't above begging. "Center, this is 36 Victor Mike. How 'bout giving us a heading through the thinnest spot in this line."

"Victor Mike, this is Center. We do not provide weather radar services. Our radar can only paint heavy precip (precipitation). Take heading one-four-five. Maintain 6,000. Keep us advised on your conditions."

Center didn't promise anything — nada. But his giving us a heading translates into, *Off the record, fellas, this looks like your best shot.* And his "Keep us advised" means, *Tell us if you make it.* The lower altitude suggests that he knows that higher altitudes usually carry more meteorological violence than lower ones. But 6,000 feet above sea level over the 4,500-foot Appalachians is a very low altitude at night, especially in a storm. The guy helped us all he could, but he promised us nothing. This is the way it's supposed to be. But you can bet your booty he's watching our blip on his radar screen right now.

Ten miles ahead — say three minutes' flying time — the lightning is fierce and active. There are very few dark areas in that wall of clouds. Everything is electrical flashes. Dark areas might be soft spots. Some pilots call them sucker holes. As we close in on the line, the flash intensity is like a giant arc welder doing stitch welds. You don't want to look at the spark. Both Pat and I slide down in our seats to keep our eyes below the glare shield. We turn the instrument lights up to full brightness. I cover my right eye with my hand in case of flash-blindness. This will give us one good eye to read the instruments if a lightning flash comes too close. The rain slams the plane all at once, and with a sudden roar. The reverberation feels like water blasts from a firehose. The turbulence picks up to a level beyond the limitations of the controls. Pat's keeping up with it pretty well. We're both cinched tight to our seats, but we're still thrown around in the cockpit. The thunder of the rain makes even shouting impossible. I bet it's hell in the back seat.

Time stops but the fury persists. We just hang on and ride it out. We have a heading, and either it's a good one or it's not. All three of us are well aware of how high the stakes are.

But the Air Traffic Controller's suggested heading turns out to be the right one. We sense we are slipping between the heaviest cells. Any of these babies is capable of shredding a little plane like a Bonanza to pieces in a heartbeat. Off both wingtips, the ferocity is even greater than what we're experiencing. We haven't been struck by lightning. I think we're between cells.

Except for the lightning flashes, the world is black. The turbulence and rain are unrelenting, but we keep plowing on. Gradually, a few of the electrical flashes move around behind us to reflect off the panel gauges. The view ahead becomes a welcoming, steady darkness. The turbulence lessens. The rain slacks off. And then, finally, little luminous lights of quiet lives appear on the earth below. The sparkles sprawl out in the valley under the nose and thin out into the black tapering profiles of the Great Smoky Mountains on our left. The dotted veins of roadways start to connect in clusters of intersecting sparkles. And then, *we're through it*!

The 145-degree heading Center gave us was a beautiful call.

And, thank goodness, the engine is still knacking away merrily. I love that sound. Don't stop knocking, trusty motor!

For the second time since we took off from Chicago, I think seriously about Zip in the back seat. Then, about that fast, I don't think about him anymore. Knowing him as I do, he's probably already worked up this elaborate story about how hard it is, in a time of need, to hit the open mouth of a Paul Masson carafe whilst penetrating a line of thunderstorms.

"Atlanta Center," Pat casually talks into his mic. "Victor Mike's with you at six [thousand feet]. We're visual, but we'll stay instruments with you to PDK."

"Roger, Victor Mike." Center then responds with measured curiosity, "How about a Pilot Report?"

Even though they could have lost us in the precipitation in the front, I bet they have a pretty damn good idea of what we just flew through. Maybe better than us.

Captain Klondike answers, "Victor Mike. Well, it did get a little bumpy there for a bit. Thanks for your help."

At least he didn't say, "Hello, Houston. We got this little red light up here … " I am really way too exhausted to laugh. There is some kind of droll collapse in the gut, and I manage only a tired smirk. Pat is fully revived and showing off his now famous SE grin to a very small and mostly disinterested audience.

This moment will become one of the benchmarks in our three lives. It is a full blown demonstration of our self-perceived invincibility. Simultaneously it is clear evidence of questionable judgment followed by improbable good luck.

The decisions made in the last 24 hours will forever be open to all kinds of criticism; all of it is valid. We took risks, and we knew we took them. But we persevered. For better or worse, the success of this flight broadens the boundaries that often limit the theater of the imagination. No matter if we were brave or foolhardy, our world, to some degree, has changed. And, in the not too distant future, those boundaries will be pushed out even further.

We land, taxi up to the Epps' terminal, and Zip emerges unsteadily from the side door of the plane. Yes, he's grinning ear to ear. It is his most infectious smile mixed with relief, gratitude and pure delight, and maybe even a little wonderment. We three grin at one another, shake hands, clap each other's shoulders, and go our separate ways. Not much is really said other than, "Good Night. See you around."

But right now, walking alone on the wet tarmac to my car, I'm what you call *spent.* All I can think about is being welcomed home, sitting in the kitchen enjoying a stack of cookies and a giant glass of milk, taking a shower, stretching out full length and closing my eyes — you know, the real stuff that makes life so good.

All three of us know that the *seed of invincibility* has been re-nourished in each of us, and all the compass needles in the world are still pointing to the Magnetic North Pole. In the next couple of years we will make two more efforts to get there, both tempting Providence every bit as much as this one.

CHAPTER 2

VIBRATIONS

ALTHOUGH IT READS like one, this memoir is not all about airplanes. It's about a few people and their relationships. It's about some ambitions, dreams, sacrifices and failures. And, in a loosely framed way, it's about their achievements and how those achievements led to other challenges.

The story just happens to involve airplanes. Besides, for flights of fancy, using airplanes just sounds right.

Also, you must remember that a fantasy mission can't be successful unless it meets three standards: the task must be fulfilled; the task must be difficult, and it must involve sacrifice. Fortunately, difficulty and sacrifice come in many flavors, and there is an abundant supply of both.

Keep in mind, too, that the fantasy-event need not to have changed the destiny of mankind in the least. However, to be considered successful, it must, at the very least, impose some measurable impact on its participants and, ideally, a few observers as well.

As described earlier, the notion of rolling the pole developed somewhat haphazardly during a lazy summer afternoon in 1978 in Oshkosh, Wisconsin. But the notion of writing about it didn't emerge for another decade and a half. This notion also happened at an airshow, but in a location much closer to home.

Were it not for the telling, this multi-year episode would have been like the tree that fell in the forest that nobody heard. And if nobody heard it, it didn't make a sound. It was only random vibrations wasting off into space. It might as well never to have happened.

But the pole-rolling thing *did* happen. And, for better or worse, please consider this account to be the sound it made. To my knowledge, except for word of mouth, the pages of Pat Epps' and my Pilot Log books, and my journals, these events have not otherwise been formally recorded.

Whoever it was who said, "Nothing is really like what it seems," didn't know much about airshows. Sometimes an airshow tries to be serious. And that's fine. But even if the theme goes folksy, or if it tries to be a little bit "carnie," it still ends up being just about the same as the serious one. And for those with even a hint of eagle blood in their veins, the similarities are a good thing.

The particular airshow that we are about to visit is a perfect example. Although Peachtree-DeKalb Airport (PDK) is not on Peachtree Street, it resides in the northeast corner of — you guessed — Atlanta, Georgia.

Now picture a beautiful, blue-sky Saturday morning in Georgia in late-May, 1998.

With free admission, you just walked right in. The parking lots were already full, and long lines of stragglers had to hike, or stroll, sometimes a mile, to get to the gate. Despite the bustle of the crowd, the overall mood, including mine, was clearly upbeat.

Several thousand of us assembled on the tarmac. Just to be in the mix of the airplanes, we got as close to the runway as the fence would allow. From there, we had perfect sight-lines for the aerial demonstrations.

At high noon, the opening ceremonies started with the traditional parachutist swirling in circles with an enormous American flag swinging a pendulum path below him. The loudspeakers over-amped the Star-Spangled Banner being sung by a young woman's brave voice. And when she hit the high note in "the land of the free" right on target, and then jumped up a full octave, the crowd cheered. Little airplanes did descending spirals around Old Glory while blowing red, white and blue smoke helices. The crowd cheered again. It never gets old. If no one was watching, I would have saluted.

Of course there were lots of rambunctious children running this way and that. In their pursuit were moms wearing baggy sweatshirts with school logos; some carried an infant under one arm and pushed a stroller with the other. There were scantily attired young beauties with flawless complexions, and there were older folks with sunburned faces and beer-bellies wandering about in walking shorts. And, of course, there were baseball caps (some worn backwards), tank tops and tee-shirts with beer ads and historic airplanes. Almost everyone had sunglasses, some docked on top of their head. Tattoos were scarce, and then only on the men. At least that's true of the tats on public display.

Lines formed to take rides in a corrugated aluminum Ford Tri-motor transport plane built in the late 1920s. War Vets in full-dress uniforms patrolled here and there like they were still on guard duty and looking for a nation to defend. Some were accompanied by Civil Air Patrol youngsters trying to look like teen-age, Field Grade officers.

And, thank goodness, there was the compelling aroma of buttered popcorn, grilling burgers, steaming hot dogs, and occasionally, a delicious whiff of aviation gas or jet fuel. Ahh, inhale deeply. It's the heady scent of an air show's Perfect Lunch.

I drove to the airport alone, snuck in a rear service gate and parked my car in a vacant space in the corner of the fuel farm. For many years I had hangared my plane here at PDK, but my financial circumstances got pretty brutal in 1992. The airplane had to go, but I kept the gate code.

The middle of the action was only a two-minute walk from the fuel farm. It's always fun to run into fellow aviators. Whether old or new, seeking the camaraderie of like-minded souls is what pilots do. It usually starts out with, "Are you still current?" That question has to do with having an up-to-date Airman's Medical Certificate and Biennial Flight Review by FAA. The answer establishes whether you are an *is* or a *was*. No matter which one you are, though, the respect still flows both ways.

When I met Chuck Dryden of the Tuskegee Airmen, I was building up my flying time at a terrific rate. He had not flown in years. He was a giant, and I a Lilliputian. Aviation, I believe, honors achievement longer than most other endeavors.

On the runway side of the display area sat a couple of old twin-engine Douglas DC-3 cargo haulers; the military calls them C-47s. They were sitting on their haunches with their noses up, sniffing the wind like a pair of giant, matched terriers. From the cockpit you could look down upon everything in the airport but the tower. Yes, I stood in that line and contributed a dollar to the cause. I talked my way into the Left Seat. Every gauge, button, lever and switch was familiar, even the smell of hydraulic fluid leaking from the valves the copilot operates to control the hydraulic system. The DC-3's cockpit plumbing recalls the cab in a steam locomotive. Seeing the instrument panel once more brought back the rich memories of both bald-faced fear and the feeling of triumph for making a successful flight out of a difficult ride.

Scattered here and there amongst the crowd were several dozen private aircraft of the popular indigenous species. Even yellow Piper Cubs had their gawkers.

Center-stage, lined up in front of the control tower, were the real superstars of the show: the War Birds. These were the ex-combat fighter planes adorned with white stars on Navy blue wings, or white stars in a blue disk on olive-drab, camouflage paint. They all had some combination of military emblems, squadron badges, stenciled numbers, battle stripes and, frequently, nose art of an almost naughty nature. Pin-up girls, as they were called during The War.

And, yes, friends, with unfettered dignity, the elegant and lethal P-51 — the Mustang — still ruled the roost.

From the take-off end of the runway could be heard the indisputable voice of authority, the sound of a thunderous and un-muffled radial engine slowly revving up to take-off power. You thought you could feel the earth tremble. At least, you wanted to think it did.

So, in general, if you like airplanes, pretty girls in short-shorts and junk food, the skeptic was wrong. This event is pretty much *exactly* like what it seems.

The actual flying part of the show started at 1:00 pm sharp. Fourth on the agenda was my old buddy, Pat Epps. He was still campaigning in his aerobatic, single engine Beechcraft Bonanza painted in all-American red, white and blue. This was the same plane in which, 22 years earlier, he had taught me how to do a proper aileron roll.

Pat gave me that lesson the day after I had dangerously botched a "self-taught" attempt to roll my own airplane, a 1963 Mooney Super 21. Thereafter, the "Super" part of my plane's designation became my airport name. You can't say I didn't warn you.

"Self-taught" means that I had read Duane Cole's book, *Roll Around a Point*. At the time, my Pilot's Log Book showed 2,135 hours as PIC (Pilot in Command). I had a Commercial License with Instrument and multi-engine ratings, so you can understand that I was way too cock-sure to ask another pilot to teach me much about anything, let alone how to do a simple roll. Besides, I was already pretty good at loops and spins. Even in those distant days, the unwritten rules concerning foolish pride were well-established.

Published in 1976, Cole's book was well-written, accurate and informative. But for a maneuver as fundamental as an airplane roll, in my ill-informed opinion, Cole expected an excessive amount of training and preparation. So I skipped the first three hours of recommended flying preparation and went directly to the explanation of how to execute a roll. It's all on page 23.

On my first attempt, while half-way through the maneuver, *and upside down*, the plane stalled and fell, inverted, out of the top of the roll. My dog Irving (a refugee from the local Pound), who had been wistfully occupying the co-pilot seat next to me, ended up (actually down) on the headliner. I tried to hold him there with my right hand while using my left hand to wrestle with the control wheel in an attempt to get the plane right-side up. The stall warning horn was blaring. I had no forward airspeed so the controls were completely limp. Then loose things started filling the cockpit. My empty coffee cup levitated into view, and then dirt off the floor came up my nose. Actually down my nose. A flight manual fluttered by, followed by my open flight case, a yellow-handled screwdriver, some pencils and my red, plastic emergency pee-bottle — luckily well-sealed with a large white cap. We were now in a sitting position but inverted, weightless, and accelerating towards Earth like Newton's apple.

The engine started over-revving past its maximum rpm redline. I had to let go of the dog to yank the throttle back to idle-cut off. With the power off but the wheels still tucked in the wings, the landing gear-warning horn then began augmenting the stall warning horn. Each horn was loud but at a different pitch. Together, their shrill warnings added a certain measure of tension. I would submit that few pilots have enjoyed both horns blowing simultaneously, upside down, for very long.

Then the outside world began to rotate to the right. These were the indicators of an inverted flat spin. Not good. An airplane must have forward airspeed for the controls to work. I immediately pushed the throttle back a full power. The gear horn went silent. For a brief second I caught a glimpse of the horizon out of the corner of my eye. That was incredibly reassuring. But then, just as suddenly, it was gone altogether. For some reason, not seeing the horizon was disproportionately worrisome. I no longer knew which way was up. The nose then began falling faster than the rest of the plane, and we began to pick up speed rapidly. The floating dirt and the rest of the stuff returned to the floor. Irving somehow came across my lap and ended up either on my feet or under the rudder pedals on my side of the plane. I couldn't tell which because my body was only loosely attached in the seat. My lap belt was clipped but not cinched down tightly — a serious oversight. Besides, with respect to Irving, I was dealing with my own life issues — not canine comfort and welfare.

Then the nose fell even more rapidly, straight down, almost to the vertical. The stall warning horn bleeped off. I pulled the control wheel full back. Simultaneously, I yanked the power off. So of course the gear horn came back on. I was late to react. We began accelerating straight down very rapidly, but maybe still a little inverted. It felt like coming down the backside of a loop and letting the speed get away from you. The Never Exceed Speed for the Mooney is noted with a red line on the airspeed indicator. That limit is 189 mph. The needle was now indicating 215 mph and climbing. The rotating, dark green, earth filled the windshield. I needed a lot of elevator and some hard right rudder to pull out of the dive and stop the rotation. From inside the plane I could not feel the spinning, but the world outside was in a wobbly orbit. I pulled back on the controls harder than I thought they could withstand. There was not much movement. Maybe an inch or two. There were only two choices. We would either auger in or come down in pieces. If the plane was going to come apart, well, it just would.

I pushed the right rudder pedal as hard as I could to stop the rotation. But being loosely secured in the seat, I didn't have good leverage. I certainly couldn't tell if I was squashing Irving or not. But if it did hurt him, he didn't let out a peep.

The only smart move I had made so far this morning was to take Duane Cole's advice about buying plenty of altitude to practice in. He recommended a minimum of 3,000 feet. I started with 7,500 feet. We used all of the former and most of the latter.

This little event did not last thirty seconds. Probably, it took half that time. But it certainly seemed longer. For some reason my mental re-plays are all in stop-action or slow motion.

Finally we started pulling out of the dive. As the airspeed bled off and dropped below redline, I added a quarter inch of throttle just to get the gear horn to shut up.

The G-forces had pulled my glasses to my lap, and from there they wormed their way down under Irving. Once back to normal speed, with the controls trimmed and the power setting brought back to cruise, I reached down and tried to haul Irv up to his former throne in the right seat. But even with a big handful of fur and skin, there was no way to get him out of the foot well. My friend was wedged in with no mind to come out. He stayed there until after we landed and the plane was shut down. I let him relax there while I tied the wings and tail down to their respective mooring rings. Once the quiet had sunk in, and his nerves got a little settled, I wriggled him out. Irving looked up at me with the widest, pleading-est eyes ever worn on a dog.

Clearly, it was at this moment that he forsook all enthusiasm in aviation. My trusting buddy's interest in sport flying was quelled — forever.

After I had the fuel truck top off the wing tanks, Irving and I drove straight over to Pat's house for a debriefing.

Pat started Epps Aviation at PDK on a shoestring budget in 1965. He and his wife, Ann, built the business in the tradition of the great American dream. It grew steadily into one of the most highly respected general aviation hubs in the country. With three youngsters, Patrick, Marion and Elaine, they settled in a comfortable, attractive and richly wooded subdivision of 1950s-vintage homes located only a few miles from the airport.

Ann answered my knock, and I met with Pat in the kitchen. Like Irving, my nerve ends were still frayed. Irving, however, went over to sniff Fuzzy, Pat's dog, and he was soon good again with the world.

As I mentioned, Pat is a people-person with a Type A personality. Most of the time he tries to hide both. I still felt compelled to spill my guts out to my friend. Atypically, he heard me out in silence. Maybe my eyes still looked like Irving's. But when I finished, he responded with sincere concern.

The drift went like this, "Glad you made it, Super. But this is basic stuff. It ain't rocket science. You lost your airspeed. Tell me, which way did you try to roll it?"

I said, "To the right."

"Well that was your first mistake." He didn't slow down, "Meet me at the airport tomorrow afternoon at four-thirty, and

I'll show you how to do it right. But I'll give you a little hint right now. Everything having to do with flying is all about airspeed. And it ain't all on the airspeed indicator dial, either. You gotta feel it. And if you don't feel it naturally, then you gotta *make* yourself feel it."

As strange as it might sound, Pat's condescending attitude was not unwelcome. It struck just the right note. The whole idea of giving a high priority to *feel the airplane* was foreign to my training. Without question, doing things by the numbers plays a big role in flying. In fact, some pilots fly only by the numbers. That was the way I was taught to fly. For years I would feel guilty if I strayed from the straight and narrow. Pat's message was that *being able to feel* is just as important, and just as legitimate.

The paradox of this lesson is that Pat is a compulsive *altitude holder*. No wandering up or down is allowed. Even if he's flying copilot, he'll reach over and tap the altimeter if it's only a little bit off the designated altitude. If you're supposed to be flying at 9,000 feet, then 8,950 is unacceptable sloppiness.

I don't know why, but I took up this almost compulsive attitude-hold idiosyncrasy. It only proves that you got to watch the company you keep.

The next day, in his red, white and blue Bonanza, Pat showed me what it feels like to set up the plane so it will want to roll itself without even taking a breath. The *numbers* are only reference points to establish what key the melody is to be played in. *Feel* is the delight of execution. With this image in mind, the transition came easily.

He taught me another thing, too. Did you know that propeller planes roll easier (faster) to the left because of the direction of the propeller's rotation? Some days later, I timed my Mooney and it took eleven seconds to roll to the right but only eight to the left. Interesting, huh?

Eventually rolls in either direction became natural and eventually lost some of their daring-do. I got so that I would roll my plane often, but only if I were alone and bored on a long flight.

Once on a long trip I got an idea. Now this is a hoot. I was alone and in the clouds on solid instruments. You couldn't see anything at all outside the cockpit: no horizon, no sun. And, except for FAA radar, nobody's watching. So I built up a little airspeed, rotated the nose up a little bit, then cranked the control wheel over to its mechanical stop and just counted. This is a maneuver you *have* to do by the numbers. I only did it once, just to see if I could. Eight seconds later, when the instruments settled, I was back at exactly my assigned altitude and heading. Air Traffic Control was none the wiser. Or at least they didn't call and ask, "November one nine two eight Yankee, we're looking at a little burble on your blip here ... "

But I have to say that it really wasn't all that much fun. It was just kind of an ultimate numbers' game to prove that it can be done. I've never tried a roll with my eyes closed, but I expect it would be about the same.

And, before I forget it, I never again rolled an airplane with my buddy Irving on board. I never want to be looked at with the eyes that looked at me that day of our flubbed, first roll attempt.

Incrementally, I added a few more maneuvers to my repertoire. But Pat moved on up to the top echelons of full-blown aerobatic performances at the national level. He's good. No, he's *very* good!

And that brings us right back to that Peachtree Airshow in May, 1998.

With the monster speakers still pumping out loud noises with a numbing beat, Pat began his airshow routine. He started with a series of graceful loops, Immelmanns, split-esses and rolls. He then climaxed the wing-over stuff with a stellar hammerhead stall. This is his favorite. I think he gets off with blood first ebbing to his head as he runs out of acceleration going straight up. Then, with just enough airspeed left to give him reliable rudder-control, he kicks the nose over to dive straight down toward earth. Then, pulling out, he has completely flushed his brain box and re-charged it with a fresh quart of re-oxygenated hemoglobin. I guess it must feel like changing the oil in your favorite car three times in an afternoon. It feels so good you just keep doing it. Or maybe it's like … well, never mind. You come up with what feels good three times in a row.

The painfully intrusive loudspeakers then switched from too-loud-rock-n-roll to too-loud announcer. But I still turn up my listening. I'm always anxious to hear about my 'ole buddy, Captain Klondike.

"Ladies and gentlemen, now performing above you is the world-famous aviator, Pat Epps. He is flying this extraordinary routine in the very same airplane that *he and some other guy* flew to the North Pole. Then they *rolled the pole!*" (Obviously, the bold italics are mine).

For some reason, I don't recall anything else the announcer had to say. I do remember that I still couldn't keep my eyes off the routine. True to form, it was flowing, graceful and, most of all, elegant. The engine sang that familiar song I had learned to respect — deep growls on climb-outs, and soothing purrs on descents. And if you listened carefully, you could hear the whistle of the slip stream singing the counter-harmony in a muffled voice. The propeller tips, as they would go supersonic, beat a timpani roll in perfect pitch.

The resulting performance was a simple, sophisticated ballet conducted at a high level of competence by the hands of a Master.

Paint splashes on canvas, dance steps on stage or music played in any key are no greater an art-form than this.

But, when it was all over, my ears still rang with the announcer's off-hand invitation to look again at an unlikely, yet perhaps, inspirational experience; summed up in the provocative phrase, "rolled the pole."

For me, memories ebbed back in a cautious and comfortable way. It was not a compelling urge to suddenly jump up and start blowing smoke and tell the story. Rather, it was a question: *Did what Pat and I worked on for two years have any meaning beyond, "You rolled the Pole? Well, how utterly useless was that?"* Yes, exactly those words have been asked.

In any event, I took the bait. I sat down and wrote this book. And if I have done my job, you might understand something about the risky compulsion to undertake a difficult and sometimes dangerous pursuit. Maybe it will make you more inclined to go chase your own will-of-the-wisp dream. Or maybe it won't. Maybe, it will make you more secure in not coloring outside the lines. Perhaps vicarious participation might be exactly all you need right now. Who knows? All I can say is, please take from this adventure all that you wish. Whatever is leftover will not go to waste.

Along the way, I trust that you will put into perspective the failures and disappointments we bore. I hope you'll pardon the tom-foolery we enjoyed, and excuse, or at least try to understand, the risks we took. And, I especially hope you'll appreciate the perseverance involved. That is much of what this book is about. If I am successful in this narrative, I hope you will respect the triumph of what can be called an adventure in full. And perhaps the sharing of the details, the blunders and the emotions of this journey will make your wildest dreams seem less wild.

There is no question that these events changed Pat's life as well as my own. It gave us sufficient experience and credentials to spend the subsequent eleven years mounting seven expeditions to find and extricate "Glacier Gal," a WWII Lockheed P-38 Lightning fighter plane, from her icy tomb 250 feet beneath the surface of the Greenland icecap.

But it is still amusing to reflect: the telling of this story all started with the annoyingly loud, *"He and some other guy…"*

CHAPTER 3

THE SECOND GO TO THE POLE

August 10, 1979

N O MATTER HOW you look at it, last year's flop at reaching the Pole is still a bitter disappointment. Despite what they say, time does not cure all ills. In fact, I'm here to tell you that for some ills, time is only an incubator.

At best, the compulsion to Roll the Pole has questionable intellectual value. I know that. It was a crazy notion to begin with — an idea born under the wing of a small plane by three grown-up guys relaxing at an air show. Some might suggest the whole willy-nilly notion should be tossed in the round file and forgotten. Many, maybe most, responsible minds would agree with that. And, I bet, they would probably get loving support for that position from spouses, family, business partners and anybody else who cared about them.

On the other hand, I cannot tell you exactly why the idea of abandoning this whole thing feels so impossible to me. But it does. A shrink would probably attribute it to my mother not breast-feeding me (I'm sure she did, but I can't remember), or my big sister, Mary Frances, taking my name away from me when I was four years old and flushing it down the toilet. She would just say "Richard" into her hand, then threw it in the bowl and flushed. Swoosh, it was gone. True story. And I can still remember bawling until my mother feigned pulling it back out, washing it in the sink, scolding my sister and giving it back to me all nice and clean. Who really knows why we do what we do, or how we feel the way we do about some things? But I do know this. For whatever reason, Rolling the Pole has worked its way very high up on my priority list. I am committed that this summer will not pass without my fulfilling this ambition.

The straight-line distance from Atlanta to the Magnetic North Pole is a little over 3,000 miles. My plane, a 1964 Mooney Super 21, is not as large, comfortable or as fast as Zip's Bonanza. Still, at an airspeed of 160 mph, a one-way trip to the Pole is a shade less than 20 hours' flying time. Throwing in some zigs and zags, headwinds and a half-dozen fueling stops, it should take about 25 flying hours to make the trip. The Mooney has a five-hour fuel endurance at cruise speed. I figure on making five, four-hour legs to reach Resolute Bay, Northwest Territories. That's the last outpost north and the jumping-off point to the Magnetic North Pole. Using these numbers, it should take two full working days to get to Resolute. Then on the third day, it would only take two hours to fly out to the Pole, spend fifteen minutes doing the aerobatic routine, and then two hours back. In zero-wind conditions, that should get me back to Resolute with forty-five minutes' fuel left in the tanks. If nothing disagreeable occurs-say, bad weather, mechanical failure, navigation glitches, or compelling distractions — I will be back in Atlanta in a week. Hardly enough time to be missed.

For some reason, there's been very little support shown for this year's trip. Can you believe that?

"Because it's there," may have been sufficient for Sir Edmund Hillary to be the first to summit Mount Everest. But this argument doesn't carry much weight with my business partners and friends in Atlanta. And it means zilch to my family.

I go through the familiar goodbye ritual at home, and Nancy reminds me of the responsibility thing.

Pat and Zip are not going this year. I'll get to that later. But right now, the Pole needs rolling, and I gotta get hustling.

At 8:13 am on August 10, 1979, Peachtree Tower clears me to taxi into position and hold. It's drizzly with wind out of the north. Finally, "November one nine two eight Yankee, cleared for takeoff. " I ease the throttle to the firewall. The engine comes up to a roar, and we're soon rumbling down the concrete runway. At 70 mph, I ease back on the control wheel.

We're swallowed by the gray overcast almost immediately.

But before I go any farther, let me clarify the "we" thing. I don't know if Lindbergh started it all, but he certainly legitimized it in his book, "We." The "we," of course, was he and his airplane, the Spirit of St. Louis. Together, they made the first solo non-stop flight across the Atlantic in 1927.

When you spend a lot of time with a machine, it is not an unnatural thing to create a certain bond or trust. I bet if a dusty old farmer who spent from first light to noon on his dirty old tractor tilling acreage, at dinner that night he would tell his wife, "Well, we finally finished the back forty and pulled over in the shade by the creek for a lunch break." The *we* thing just feels natural. Yes, the farmer or the pilot may be without other human company, but there is still a lot going on between the two parties in attendance.

Now getting back to why we are flying through Canada today. The weather briefing this morning predicted solid overcast, intermittent rain, moderate turbulence, and a 15 to 20-knot headwind.

The headwind is forecast to continue all the way to the Great Lakes.

Because winds aloft usually increase with altitude, I file for only 6,000 feet. It's hand-flying all the way. Actually, it's more like arm-wrestling all the way. The headwind slows my ground speed down to 125 miles per hour, about that of a Cessna trainer.

I refuel in Louisville, Kentucky. It's pouring rain. Getting wet is a given, But the bigger bugger is allowing water in the gas tanks. The filler caps are on the top of the wings. This is never fun. I file another Instrument Flight Plan to Thunder Bay, Canada. Flight Service weather forecasts haven't changed; they're still calling for rain, clouds, turbulence and headwinds.

Nail-biting adventure, this is not. Tedium, it is a lot of.

Passing through Chicago airspace, Air Traffic Control gives me headings right up the centerline of Lake Michigan. The lake-effect breaks up the clouds a little, at least enough to let me look upon what seems like an ocean. There are no visible shorelines. It feels like I'm in the eye of a hurricane: serene and alluring, but surrounded by apprehension. Who would have thought to bring a life raft?

The glimpse of sky only lasts a few minutes. Then the overcast returns, and we're tucked right back in the clouds again.

My trusty Mooney has a cabin about the size of an old VW Beetle. After our twelve years of flying together, it fits like a second skin. I can sense every smell, sound or vibration in this plane. Although I'm not sure if it has the same feelings for me, I still believe we have an enduring friendship. It goes back to the *we* thing.

At our cruise speed of 160 miles per hour, we're getting about 20 miles per gallon. Because of its reputation for being a little twitchy to fly, Mooney installed an automatic wing-leveler as standard equipment in this model. If you let go of the controls, this device brings the plane back to level. For reasons unknown, this plane is the only Mooney I've ever heard of that doesn't have one. It's one of a kind. I like that.

Coming up on Green Bay, the weather eventually lifts. Visibility goes from nothing to 50 miles of freshly rained-upon, pungent, deep-green Wisconsin farmland. It's all in National Geographic-exaggerated color. With the bad weather behind me, I cancel my Instrument Flight Plan. Finally, I'm a man alone. I need this. The air either smells really good up here, or I just think it smells good. It's also time for a mood change. I'm really tired to the core of being abused by Mother Nature.

The headwinds have already added an hour to my flight time. This puts Thunder Bay just out of fuel range. Iron Mountain airport comes up under the nose. I call their Tower, get a clearance to land, bank left and line up on the active runway. After I touch down and switch to Ground Control, they direct me to their small terminal. Perhaps it's the architect in me, but there is something appealing about the scale of the building. I get the feeling it is a three-quarter scale model of a big city terminal. The lobby is devoid of people. Maybe they don't fit.

So far today I've flown seven hours and 45 minutes. The headwind has been relentless.

I'm now sitting here in the scaled down waiting room at the Ford Airport in Iron Mountain, Michigan, munching crackers and drinking a Coke. I'm bushed to the bone. My motivation needle is barely twitching. I'd give anything for a quick nap, but this lobby doesn't feel much like a recharging station. Somebody might walk in, and if that happens there are not enough people for anonymity.

But, while I'm sitting, let me take a minute to get back to why Pat and Zip aren't here. A month ago, I asked each of them to come along on this junket. Zip thought it was a crazy idea and said he had better things to do. Pat is building a new passenger terminal for his aviation business at PDK. The design of the Epps Terminal is one of my firm's proudest architectural achievements. The building is now in the middle of its construction phase. When I invited Pat to come along on this trip, he said, "No. Not this time. I'm going to stay here and finish this job. But if you have to go, you go ahead."

Was there a little edge to, "if you have to go"?

Yes.

Does that bother me?

Sure, a little. But Pat totally understands. We didn't need to talk about it.

But what I feel most guilty about is leaving all the construction decisions in other people's hands while I fly off to tilt at windmills. So, you ask, *do idle compulsions outweigh professional responsibility?*

Apparently, sometimes they do.

Refueled and back up at 7,500 feet I head north and fly across Lake Superior to Thunder Bay, Canada. I'm still bone weary, but the flight is not even 200 miles and the visibility continues to be postcard perfect. After the day I've been through, this weather is way too pretty to talk with Air Traffic Controllers. So I fly visually without a flight plan. Ten miles out from Thunder Bay, I see the airport and radio Approach Control. They ask my intentions. I tell them I want to land. But I'm thinking to myself, *Dummy, what do you think I want to do? I filed an International Flight Plan to land here before I left this morning.*

Over the mic I tone it down to, "Two eight Yankee. Landing Thunder Bay."

"November 1928 Yankee, we do not have a Flight Plan on file for you to enter Canada."

Well, damnation. Now who's the dummy? It never occurred to me that my "Request for Customs" was voided when I cancelled my Instrument Flight Plan back at Ford Airport. I know better than this. Right now, I'd like to blame fatigue. But really, it's just a dumb-ass mistake.

"Roger, Thunder Bay. Two eight Yankee. May I request a special entry?" I have no idea if anything like this even exists. But it can't hurt to ask. I'm already thinking I might have to go back to Iron Mountain, land, and re-file a flight plan with a request for Customs.

Approach Control politely obliges me and gives me the radio frequency for the tower. I switch to tower. They clear me to land and then give me the frequency for Ground Control. I twist the dials again and call Ground. A polite voice directs me to taxi to the most remote corner of the airfield—near the trees on the desolate side of the runway. I'm told to park there, shut down, and wait for a customs agent to arrive. Then, in a stiffer tone, the voice adds, "Sir, do not leave your airplane." It is not a gentlemen's request.

"Roger, two eight Yankee."

It has been a long, tense day. This wait-time is relaxing and passes quickly enough. I think I need it.

After five minutes, though, I get antsy. So I open the door, climb out on the wing and step down on the concrete apron to stretch my legs. The Man didn't say I couldn't get out. He just said don't leave. I'll bet you anything that the guys in the tower are watching with binoculars, so I probably shouldn't relieve myself while I'm doing time here in the isolation box.

An hour and a half later a customs inspector drives up in a pickup truck with a royal pomp and circumstance insignia on the door. He's wearing a dress blue uniform, and he looks like an arresting officer as he approaches the plane in long, purposeful strides.

I ask myself why in the name of hell I had to get out of the airplane? At least I didn't pee.

The officer is not smiling.

Although he looks about forty, he's one of those rosy-cheeked guys with bright curiosity in his eyes. His mouth, however, is set in a straight, horizontal line. I can't read him. But in the few words it takes to ask for my passport, he comes across as courteous and respectful. There's a friendly cadence in his speech pattern. Each word has a little different note like a TV reporter.

I keep waiting for it, but he doesn't mention my Request for Entry blunder. To me, it is a conspicuous omission. It keeps me on edge. The officer looks under the seats and in the baggage compartment just like he's supposed to. But overall, he gives the plane only a little more attention than the casual once-over we got last year. When I answer the "Sir, what is your destination?" question, with "The Magnetic North Pole," he studies me more carefully. Our eyes really lock for the first time. I think he thinks maybe I'm joshing, but he's not entirely certain. The officer then gives another quick look around the cockpit. I can't help wondering what is going through his mind. Maybe I look suspicious. I do wear a full beard. I know damn well I'm red-eyed. And I did enter Canada in a really dippy manner.

As he finishes writing up my Certificate of Entry, I ask about the cost of this special reception. He smiles and says, "There is no cost, sir. Welcome to Canada. I trust you will find your Pole."

From the tone of his voice, I can't help but substitute "senses" for "Pole." After the officer drives away, I taxi the plane back across the airport to the tie-down/re-fuel apron.

Whew. I'm in!

The motel is part of the airport's administration complex. It's functional, clean and contains a noisy bar. This is perfect. The call home is answered every bit as courteously as the Customs inspector's greeting.

"Mitch?" She was Nancy Mitchell before we were married. "I'm in Thunder Bay, Ontario. The plane's running fine, and I'm at the Valhalla Inn here in the airport." (Isn't Valhalla where Norsemen go when they die?). I give her the motel telephone number and my room number. If there is coolness in her reply, I don't hear it. Even though I've only been gone twelve hours, it seems like a week. I want to hear all about the kids. Nancy is both generous and patient in giving a full report on all those wonderful, inconsequential things children do that mothers like talking about and daddies like to hear.

She ends the conversation with, "Keep in touch. Call me if you need some help. We expect you back in good shape."

Dinner is a hamburger and fries at the bar. Neither is as salty and greasy as back in Georgia, but they're still okay. The too-much Heinz catsup tastes exactly the same.

It's been a year since Zip, Pat, and I were limping back to Atlanta with the engine knocking and our tails dragging. I can still feel the leftover anxiety in the air.

Even with crazy, ill-defined apprehensions swirling around in my head, I write up these notes. For me, there is something relaxing about keeping a journal. It's spool-down time. It lets me bag up little packages of anxiety or pleasure that can be unzipped years later. Most of the time, they still have a little smell left in them.

So, friendly reader, although the sun is still up, I say good night.

An hour after first light, I'm in the air and headed north. The weather is beautiful with the sun reflecting off the right wing. The fresh air vent is wide open. The 350 miles to Big Trout Lake pass quickly. Big Trout's a remote, sub-arctic paradise with seaplanes, airplanes, powerboats, four-wheelers and comfortable, well-built cabins surrounding a large crystal blue lake. Thick Canadian forests and dense green vegetation overflow to the edge of the shoreline everywhere. It smells clean and fresh.

The Mooney's fuel tanks get topped off, my stomach is restocked with crackers, nuts and a Coke, and I'm off and north-bound again. Things are looking up. I'm finally feeling like I'm getting into this thing. The winds aloft are off the left wing, but thankfully with no headwind component.

The next 400 miles to Churchill should take about three hours and 20 minutes. As I work my way north, the crummy weather gradually returns. An hour out of Big Trout Lake we are back on solid instruments in soggy cloud. I get no peek at what this part of Canada looks like. Last year it was dense forests and sparkling lakes. This year it is likely still dense forests and sparkling lakes, but all I can see is solid cloud and steady rain. After the first hour, I am out of range of all radio contact, navigation beacons and visual references. It's now solely a matter of flying magnetic compass headings. Canada just gets bigger, lonelier and darker while I get smaller, lonelier and darker.

The magnetic compass seems to be losing whatever crispness it previously had. Even though I hold the plane straight with wings level, the compass heading will gradually rotate to the left. If I wait a minute or two, it will eventually wander back.

Another hour passes. The view from the plane stays the same, which is to say, none. There is only grey-white cloud. I pass the time by watching the altimeter, the airspeed indicator, the compass, the artificial horizon and the panel clock. Only the clock moves. There is no sense of motion. I am suspended in space, and the world may or may not be turning below me.

Oops, there's a little glitch.

The fuel gauge needle for the left wing tank hasn't moved since Big Trout Lake. This is not good. I'm flying on that tank, and the needle is still pegged at "full." Back in the States, with refueling opportunities everywhere, this would be more of an annoyance than a problem. Fortunately I've caught it early in this leg. It may be as simple as a loose wire on the sender. To remind myself to look at it in Churchill, I stick a yellow Post-It on the panel next to the gauge. If I can't fix it, I'll use this tank for takeoff and then run it dry. You know it's empty because the engine sputters. I'll note its time-duration and then set a timer. I'll then watch the right gauge to keep up with fuel remaining. This is not ideal, but turning back because of one fuel gauge problem seems a little over-cautious at this point. You agree up there, don't you?

At two hours and 33 minutes, right on time, the engine stumbles. I switch to the right tank and the motor comes right back to life. Perfect. I know I have two and a half hours (plus a few minutes) left and a good gauge to monitor it.

Depending upon the altitude of the plane, line-of-sight radio navigation extends about 60 to 100 miles out from the transmitting beacon. We are now way beyond that. As a secondary navigation instrument, I have an Automatic Direction Finder (ADF). This is a radio receiver that will pick up both navigation beacons and commercial AM radio stations from distances over the horizon. But right now it's not acting right. The only radio station I can pick up is both very weak and 90 degrees to the right of where my navigation says it should be. Hmm, decision time again.

This one's easy. I'm not going to turn around. I'm going to Churchill, come hell or high water.

What I need right now is a big target to fly to. So I ease the nose another 45 degrees to the right and take a full easterly course in hopes of hitting the Hudson Bay. This body of water is larger than all the Great Lakes combined. Even without a compass or navigation instruments, by flying relative to the muted sun, I ought to be able to find something this big. The clock is coming up on noon, so by flying due east, even without a compass, the sun will be directly off the right wing. This is caveman navigation, so you know it works.

The minutes pass slowly and nothing changes but the hands on the clock and the needle on the one working fuel gauge. This affords more than ample time to get myself all worried-up.

As I think about it, the radio problem looms larger than the fuel gauge issue. I suspect that navigation in the polar region will **not** include the magnetic compass. I don't know how I'm going to do it, but I do know one thing for sure: I haven't the slightest idea what the hell a magnetic compass will do over the Magnetic

North Pole. At this point, the upside down thing is way off my mental radar screen.

To keep everything in proper order, I am only certain of three things: the ADF radio has a problem, the magnetic compass is going soft, and one fuel gauge is inoperative. This is not a lot of worry. But it's also not inconsequential. Aircraft disasters are seldom the result of a single problem. They're almost always the consequence of several contributing factors working in collusion with one another.

After a little more than two hours of studying nothing outside the cockpit but the wing tips and propeller blur, I break out of the clouds. It happens with a gentle softening of the clouds and then the sunshine working its way in. It's nothing like the colorful explosion of Wisconsin farmland we had yesterday. But, I'll tell you for certain, it's every bit as welcome.

Then, right there beneath the nose, emerges what looks like the Atlantic Ocean. You cannot see the opposite shore. Of course it's not the ocean. It's pay dirt; the Hudson Bay. And it's exactly what we need right now.

The shoreline has neither beaches nor cliffs, and there is certainly no sign of human intervention. The great Canadian tree-line must bend up to the lake. I see what I would guess to be trees and tundra running irregularly along the shoreline. From the coast line looking east, the world turns into reflective water that extends beyond the horizon 40 or 50 miles away. There is no surf at the shore line, nor is there any apparent wave action off-shore. It's just a huge body of pure, placid and highly reflective water.

The sky over the bay is medium blue, and the water mirrors it like a looking glass. The surface is so smooth you can see the reflections of every scattered cloud just above the horizon.

Matching up the coast with my charts shows that I am nearly 100 miles off course. My built-in error should have put me about 30 miles off, just enough to be able to see the airport. This is a worrisome difference. Part of the difference is that I choked and headed due east looking for the Bay. Unfortunately this also gives me a strong message that the magnetic compass is only marginally reliable at latitudes this far north.

But there's no turning back now. The mental disconnect from the safe and comfortable life back in the lower Forty-Eight is complete. The rules of safety and convention have changed. I am beyond the point of no return. I am confident now that I _will_ find the Pole, and I _will_ roll it.

Flying visually up the coast, Churchill eventually rolls into view. The Control Tower clears me to land on their two-mile long runway. This is longer than the space shuttle runway at Cape Canaveral. I fly the first mile and a half down the runway at 20 feet, then land near the far end. The airport is immense. Obviously, it is a former military installation that was probably really important at one time. There are still dozens of huge gunmetal gray buildings lined up on both sides of vast concrete aprons. Before I land, I can see the road that runs from the airport to town and another road that goes from there out to what must be the city land-fill. There is a cluster of huge grain elevators in town, so there must be a railroad. I say that because other than the one to the airport and the other to the dump, I see no roads leading in or out of town.

As I approach the end of the runway, I quit sightseeing and land the plane in the last few hundred yards. I should have gone around. No, I should have paid a little more attention to flying instead of skylarking. But I land firmly, brake hard and no harm done. Ground Control doesn't call, so I use the closest taxiway to backtrack to the airport facilities. Rolling up to the buildings, I see no signs of human habitation. There are no people, no trucks or cars, no equipment and certainly no stacks of goods. There isn't even any trash.

This is spooky. Down here, as I taxi between the hangars, I cannot even see the tower. I continue to drive the Mooney around what looks like an abandoned airport in a science fiction movie. I feel a little like a cockroach sniffing for crumbs in hidden places.

Finally, way in the back of the second row, I come up on a hangar with large, open doors. Its nose protruding like a bear coming out of hibernation is a huge, grungy Curtiss C-46 Commando cargo plane. It's a World War II-era monster, apparently still making a living in the Arctic hinterland. That's civilization enough for me. I park in the lee of the building, shut the motor down and chock the wheels.

The sudden absence of engine roar makes me close my eyes and take a deep breath. What a relief! The Arctic air lacks any trace of the pungent, pollen-rich stuff we inhale back home. If Southern air doesn't actually have calories in it, I'll still bet it's full of carbohydrates.

As I snoop through the back rooms of the hangar, I hear two male voices talking in a maintenance office. I stick my head through the door and knock on the jamb. When they look my way, I ask, "You guys mechanics?" The older, saltier of the two, still looking at me, takes his time and slowly replies, "That's a negative."

There it is. In those words, he's said it all. He's the pilot of the C-46. His angular posture and tobacco-rich tone of voice tell me that he knows how to get around the Northwest Territories with the best of them. He's the picture of confidence. I know right away that he's the guy I'm looking for. Now, if I just don't screw it up, I'll be navigating in no time.

If Captain Klondike were here, he'd just walk in, pull up a chair, sit down with these guys, turn on his SE grin, ask them for a cup of coffee and start telling a totally irrelevant story about how his great-grandmother's spinster sister had the first bicycle in Dahlonega, Georgia. And how she put a homemade magnetic compass on the handlebars right next to the acetylene headlamp that every bicycle had in those days. In ten minutes, they'd all be buddies for life. In another ten minutes, they'd have the compass out of the airplane doing whatever you do to make compasses work better.

But I ain't Epps. Not even close. I can only do the best I can do. And the pity of it is that I have to think about it.

Consciously, I want to minimize my ignorance of Arctic navigation, but I don't really don't know how to do that. So I come straight to the point. This is so un-Eppsonian. I explain the wandering compass and faulty ADF navigation problems of the last few hours. The man sitting next to the pilot is a mechanic; he rotates a piece of equipment the size of a generator he's working on and looks engaged. The pilot listens, but with what looks like an edge of boredom. When he finally stands up and fieldstrips his cigarette butt, it's the clear practice of an old but unforgotten sense of military discipline. He's a little gaunt, and he has a three-day beard. He's wearing a faded baseball cap, a denim jacket and jeans, and work boots. Surprisingly, he's not wearing the metal-rimmed sunglasses that are the signature eyewear of so many pilots (and pilot wannabes). The overall impression is that he's more than a little worn.

I feel that I'm being respectful to a fault. It's distancing us. The buddy-buddy thing isn't even close to working.

Eventually, almost reluctantly, he agrees to come out and look at my plane. This might appear like a little thaw in the relationship, but he knows who is boss here. We both do. He struts. I just walk briskly.

When we get to the plane, the lecture begins. "First off, you got no business flying that damn little puddle-jumper up here. You understand that? And second, I'd just take that piece of shit compass out and throw it out the window. Far as I'm concerned, they're just a distraction and give you more trouble than they're worth." He pauses. I don't answer. I don't know how to be conversational with all this. Then he goes on. "Hell. I wouldn't throw it out the window; but I'd throw it under the seat…or in the trash!" Maybe throwing things out the window gave him second thoughts about the environment.

Of course this is not at all like anything I want to hear. I asked for a little help from a fellow aviator and, so far, all I've gotten is dissatisfaction and condescension. This is not a good start. Where's Klondike when I really need him?

When I tell him about my idea of rolling the pole, his response is silence. Kind of like the Customs Officer at Thunder Bay. Now I'm thinking that the pilot and that Thunder Bay customs officer and I may be of entirely like mind: I am in way over my head on this thing.

I go back to basics, "Well, you may be able to navigate without a compass, but I gotta have one." The pilot shrugs and doesn't respond. He's going to make me beg.

I ask, "Okay, if you don't have a compass, how do you know which way is north?"

"Simple, you just take sun shots."

"I know you're not going to believe this, but I didn't bring either a sextant or sun tables. Can I buy them in Churchill?"

"You don't need to. You have a plastic protractor don't you?"

"Sure." I answer, and thank goodness for small favors. In my flight case I have a three-inch diameter, plastic protractor used for measuring course angles on charts.

"Alright, you have a toothpick, don't you?"

"No." Damn. I'm now back to zero.

"Well here, take mine and I'll show you something. This might just save your ass someday."

He pulls a worn, probably used, toothpick out of his jacket pocket. "Stick this toothpick in the center of that protractor to form a sundial. Next, multiply Greenwich Mean Time by fifteen and then subtract your longitude. Calculate the reciprocal of that number and put the shadow of the toothpick on that new number and your protractor is oriented to TRUE north. Plug that into your directional gyro and you're good for fifteen minutes."

The pilot went on to share a few flying tales about using this sun compass. If I retold these stories here, your eyebrows would raise and your eyelids would lower. But here, at the feet of the Master, I listen intently and I believe his every word.

Our relationship may have softened a little since my unfortunate, "Are you guys mechanics?"

So I press a little more. Not wanting to appear too stupid, but needing to know, I ask, "Now that I don't need a compass anymore, what if I wanted to fix that old piece of shit compass in my airplane just for the hell of it?"

"Simple. First you take the cover off the face of the compass. That'll expose two small brass screws. Taxi out and orient the plane pointing to magnetic north on the north-south runway. You do know that the numbers on the end of the runways are its magnetic heading, don't you? Then you adjust the left screw so that you take out half of the error. Reverse the plane to face south and repeat the process. Take out half the error. Then do the whole thing again on an east-west runway with the right screw. The key is to take your time and keep taking out only half the error. This is called "swinging the compass." Eventually you'll get it to where you want it. You'll need a non-ferrous screwdriver to do this. Like brass. You got one, don't you?"

"Well, no, actually I don't."

"Figures. Come on back to the shop."

The "figures" keeps me in my place. And, yes. I knew about the numbers on the end of the runway. It just seemed wiser to take the hit and not say anything.

This whole drill with the pilot is far from easy. He's got me eating crow with a pitch fork. But in terms of information, I'm a sponge and he's a Professor Emeritus in the Fundamentals of Primary Navigation giving a post-graduate course in Arctic survival. If I had to, I'd eat more than crow to keep this thing going.

Like all valuable lessons the tuition ain't cheap. Either I pay for it here with humility, or I pay for it out there somewhere with I'd hate to think what.

The Pilot rummages through a desk drawer and then hands me an exquisitely machined brass screwdriver. The tool is about half the diameter of a yellow wooden pencil and as long as a Marine Band harmonica. The shank is stainless steel. I try to pay for it, but there's no way. The pilot eventually reveals his name: Don Bennett. But to me, he will always be The Pilot. I spend another full hour with him reviewing magnetic variation, deviation, compass procession rates, preferred communication frequencies and, of course, ditching procedures. This is stuff you can't buy.

This time that Don is giving me will always be one of those never-forgotten few hours in my life. He becomes the guardian angel who appears at exactly the right moment to prepare you for the next leg of a spiritual journey. This whole afternoon's experience is somewhere between mythical and, if you will, Divine.

What started earlier today as a chilly rebuff turns into paternal patience. We are actually clicking. No. It's more than clicking. I don't know when it happened but right now we're together on that special wavelength that people very rarely find. It must have happened when I got lost in the lessons and stopped trying to defend my ignorance.

Then, quickly, The Pilot looks at his watch, jumps up and says, "I gotta go. Come on. Come with me. I wanna show you something."

The other guy, the mechanic, has been sitting there at a work table tinkering with the mystery gizmo and watching the lesson in silence. The Pilot says, "See ya," to him as he heads to the door. The mechanic doesn't speak to either one of us. He just smiles generously and nods like this happens all the time. I think he completely understood the intellectual metamorphosis that took place in only a couple of hours.

We brisk-walk, pace for pace this time, over to the C-46, and climb into the cargo hold. Don leads me up the steeply inclined floor to the cockpit. Scattered around the seats and the floor are slips of paper bearing phrases like "10.30x15=154.50-95 … "

Hanging on the throttle quadrant is a pair of aviator Ray-Bans. Oh, and I forgot to mention The Pilot's watch. Yes, it has a big black face with lots of dials and buttons on the side. My hero's image is now complete and perfectly composed in every respect. For some reason I'm just happy as hell.

But right now, Don has already pissed away too much time with me and is anxious to get going. I return aft and swing the huge cargo door closed from the outside. Don latches it from the inside. I move around to stand in front of each engine with a fire extinguisher as he cranks it up. I'm in goosebumps as each of the C-46's 18-cylinder, 2,000 horsepower Double Wasp radial engines come thundering to life. When they are both running smoothly, and the exhaust is blowing clear, I give him a thumb's up. Don throws a casual salute. I salute back and try to look equally casual. And then, carefully at first, he rumbles out of the hangar and onto the tarmac: a solo pilot in a 35-year-old monster metal bird. There is no copilot, no navigator, no compass, and no sweat. He's The Pilot.

Of course, Don is absolutely correct. Some of what he has taught me today will save my ass on more than one occasion in the future.

But you gotta hang on, up there. We'll get to all that soon enough.

After Don is out of sight, I spend the next two hours swinging the compass, but I can never eliminate all of the error. Certain headings stay inconsistent. Well, maybe The Pilot's right about its usefulness; maybe I won't need it after all.

Back in the hangar office, I ask the mechanic if I can telephone for a taxicab to come pick me up and run me the four miles in to town.

Check-in at the lackluster Arctic Inn takes two minutes. "Sign here, that'll be thirty bucks." Before I go out to hunt for food, I dutifully record today's remarkable ground school in my journal. It's ironic. In high school I hated doing homework, especially if it had to do with writing. So most of the time, I didn't. I just took the hits and got bad grades. Funny how some things can come back and bite you.

Churchill is a "dry" town, so I settle for an overcooked hamburger and a sorta-cold Coke at a local family's three-table restaurant. Calling the States requires my going to a telephone office and asking an operator for help. I've done enough of that already today, so I opt out. Besides, I'm not feeling all that enthused about tomorrow's flight north. I understand the physics of the sun-compass thing, but if that really is all I have to navigate with to make this last fifteen hundred miles to the Pole, I have to wonder about the wisdom of the undertaking. There are still some loose ends to tighten up. Besides, I just called last night.

I spend a fitful night in my nicotine-laced motel room. Smoking seems to be a national past time up here.

It's now a new morning, but for some reason I feel a little low-spirited. Dammit. I should have called home last night. Yesterday's burst of energy has faded somewhat, and now I'm not at all into charging further north. The gray overcast, cold winds and rain contribute to the gloominess. Walking around in the town's muddy streets in a failed quest for breakfast doesn't help either. I'll eat crackers, Cokes, and nuts later in the plane. This is the third day of this trip, and I'm still having problems adjusting to loneliness. Two days is about my average for solitude-correction, and it needs to start going away soon. It saps energy. But most of all, I'm simply tired of it.

I start walking to the airport, but within ten minutes I'm offered a ride by a maintenance guy who's going out there to prepare a building for the winter.

After thanking him for the lift I go to the Flight Services Office to check on the weather. Churchill is clearing, and the forecast is for scattered clouds extending 400 miles north to an Inuit village called Baker Lake; it's about 750 miles from there to Resolute. My plan for today is to refuel there and then press on. The weather at Resolute is overcast with a 100-foot ceiling and quarter-mile visibility. It's holding steady, and this is not good. That ceiling is only half the minimum required for an instrument approach. We need a 200-foot ceiling. I hate pushing ahead knowing I can't land at Resolute. On the other hand, even my sagging motivation tells me I've got to keep going.

Remember last year, pressing on with a knocking engine? That set the bar pretty high for finking out because of a little bad weather.

Just a few minutes after takeoff, the weather starts improving, and so does my attitude. What a relief. I was afraid that I was going to have to live with me like this all day. The engine sounds solid and willing. I just found the Post-It note reminding me to work on the fuel gauge. It must have fallen off the panel when I was swinging the compass. But the compass does seem to be working a bit better.

For nearly 100 miles, I fly north at 200 feet along the western shoreline of the Hudson Bay. I'm looking for polar bears on the left and white Beluga whales on the right. There's no luck with either. I drop a little lower. The bay looks clear and quite shallow. The bottom sand shows the flow of currents and eddies. The tundra and lichen on the left are dull except for the million lakes everywhere. Life looks sparse and tenuous on both sides of the shoreline.

Per yesterday's schooling, I take a sun shot every 15 minutes during the first hour. They work perfectly. I love doing it. I'm still emotionally dependent on my magnetic compass, but now I can relegate it to backup status. Well, a backup for only as long as I have a sun to shoot. If I have to fly through cloud banks for any length of time, I lose the sun. Then I'm back on the mag-compass for primary navigation. The compass is still not as stable as it should be. It wanders less seriously than it did yesterday, but it still wanders.

I'm getting the notion that navigation is going to become much more of an issue than I had ever imagined back in Atlanta. Well, the truth of the matter is, I didn't know enough about it to even imagine what navigation would be like up here. I guess that's what I'm doing now — figuring it out.

There's another half an hour of tolerable weather, then I'm back in the clouds again. This is not good.

Because the Mooney has no autopilot, flying requires constant attention. Every minute is comprised of an instrument scan of altitude, attitude, airspeed, engine monitoring, and navigation. At normal cruise speed, this only takes a couple of seconds every half minute or so.

This leaves plenty of unused brain cells available for contemplating loneliness, anticipating predictable problems and imagining unexpected ones we don't have yet — and may never have. But you gotta think about something. That's the way we're wired.

At two hours and 26 minutes out of Churchill, the engine sputters and I switch tanks. It fires right back up again. I note the time on my kneepad. The left fuel tank is now dry. The right one is full. I have another two and a half hours of fuel (minus four minutes). Who needs a stinking gas gauge anyway?

I calculate that it's another hour and a half to Baker Lake. This leaves an hour of reserve fuel. That seems like a surplus of plenty, except when you figure in my navigation issue. If we don't find Baker Lake, we don't have enough fuel to fly to any alternate destination. See what I mean about worrying about things that don't need worrying about? When we left Churchill, Baker's weather was forecast to be above minimums. The current solid cloud bank shouldn't last too much longer. I climb up to 13,000 feet to see if I can get on top for sun shots.

At 13, no joy. Solid soup. I ease back down to 9.

Canada is enjoying one big mother cloud cover, I'll tell you that. I sure hope they're right about Baker Lake's weather.

On a couple of occasions in the past I've taken this plane up to 17,000 feet without oxygen. Obviously, that's not such a hot idea, and you don't want to stay there very long if you do. At higher altitudes, the winds frequently increase, so there's the risk of getting caught in a jet stream blowing us who knows where. Without reference to the terrain below, there is this crazy notion that I'm flying 165 miles per hour northwest and the jet stream is blowing 165 miles per hour southeast. This would leave me suspended in space and just burning fuel. Without visual reference or radio navigation, there is no sensation of movement. Again, the only things moving are the hands on the panel clock and the right fuel gauge.

Then, in the middle of my little worry bubble, the OMNI needle wiggles! This is the line of sight, primary navigation instrument that will steer us directly to Baker Lake. My eyes stay glued to the instrument looking for another movement of even the faintest magnitude. It jiggles again but takes several more minutes to completely come to life. Now I will need neither the sun nor the magnetic compass to get us there. We're golden!

With the navigation link restored, my confidence level roars back *con gusto.*

I've got plenty of fuel, and the OMNI needle is locked onto Baker Lake. The rest is a cakewalk. On the negative side, however, I didn't pick up their long-range ADF radio signal. Given the uncertainty of my magnetic compass, this instrument is essential to finding Resolute, the last airport between me and the Pole. Maybe the ADF transmitter at Baker Lake isn't working. I will surely remember to ask the airport radio operator about this. How about you up there? Maybe you'll remind me to ask when I check the weather, ok?

In any event, I'm plenty happy to make this important way-point. This is the last stop before the long leg to Resolute. If I can get there tonight, maybe I can fly to the Pole tomorrow. Worse case, I'll sit there for a few days and wait for good flying conditions. I only need one clear day to do the deed.

Baker Lake is about 150 miles south of the Arctic Circle. Its gravel strip is 4,000 feet long, and the landing is a breeze. At the fuel pump I ask the Inuit attendant to top off both tanks. He smiles obligingly. He should. Aviation gas costs $5.00 per gallon here—twice what it costs in the States—and he only accepts cash.

The town is a scattering of several dozen one-story, cement block buildings laced together with heavy electrical wire-webbing held aloft by long, angular wooden power poles. The unattractive wiring grid dominates the townscape. Snowmobiles and four-wheelers are the transportation devices of choice. They are parked randomly at almost every steep-roofed, wooden house. The streets are gravel, and there is an abundance of trash everywhere. A tidy village this is not. The weather station is literally a walk-in cooler, complete with a refrigerator door fitted with a chrome handle and hinges. The foot-thick walls of solid insulation are sparingly perforated with a few small, square triple-glazed glass windows that don't open.

The meteorologist, a self-described, "Torontoan doing time in Purgatory," says he has no weather report from Shepard Bay, but Resolute is now overcast with a 400-foot ceiling, light snow and a quarter-mile visibility. Resolute is 750 miles north, about the distance from Atlanta to New York. With no wind, the range of the Mooney is about 900 miles. This leaves nearly an hour's fuel reserve. The nearest alternate, Shepard Bay, is 350 miles from there. Consequently, if I fly to Resolute and can't land, there will be some tough decisions to make. Well, that's not exactly true. It means that if we get to Resolute, and it's below landing minimums, there is no choice but to land there anyway. The man in Purgatory offers, "The weather office for Shepard Bay is closed today but will be open tomorrow, if that helps. But I heard that they are either low or they're out of avgas. Can you use auto gas?"

"I don't know. Maybe. In an emergency, I probably could for a short flight. Right now I will keep it only as a last ditch option."

Another choice, of course, is to stay here overnight. A better forecast for Resolute would certainly cheer things up. But the reality is I'm in a serious go-mode and pushing hard. I only hope it's not too hard. The sun will not set in Resolute for another week, so darkness isn't an issue. Sitting around here swatting mosquitoes in this outpost on the tundra is already driving me crazy. Actually, you don't swat mosquitos here. There are too many. You wipe them off. They're everywhere. If you take a deep breath, you get a protein boost.

Over-nighting here is just not on my emotional agenda. I have plenty of energy left, the plane is fueled up, and there's a cardboard box half-full of junk food and a cooler with plenty of Cokes. Plus, there are four cans of warm beer in the back seat.

But, most of all, I feel that I have to make things happen. You can't do that sitting here in Nowhere, Northwest Territories.

Borrowing from old fighter pilot gargon, *I kick the tires and light the fires.*

With Baker Lake thirty minutes behind me, I'm back in the same old solid cloud bank again. There is no visibility. The OMNI beacon has dropped off, so now I'm back to navigating with my somewhat less than entirely reliable magnetic compass.

Man, I hate this. What was I thinking getting back into these clouds?

There is no radio contact with anyone.

There is no sun to shoot.

And there are no alternate airports.

The cabin heater control is full-on, and it's still cold. I break out my parka, which is hard as hell to wrestle into in the Mooney's cramped cockpit. In another thirty minutes it starts to snow. It's dark enough for the landing light in the nose to reflect off what becomes a tunnel of sparkling streaks of white-light. The silver veins follow the slipstream of the plane perfectly. But it's directly in front of the nose that is the most fascinating. I'm perpetually flying into a tunnel. None of it sticks to the plane; at zero degrees

Fahrenheit outside, it's too cold. But it is intoxicating to watch. Even though I know I'm probably hours out of range, I keep fiddling with the radio to pick up Resolute. I sure would like to connect with mankind somehow.

But there is no connection. I am a dark particle floating in a white, ice-crystal space.

After another thirty minutes of solid instrument flying, I'm slipping back into my worry mode. It's been over an hour without a sun shot. The direction of my flight is based only on estimates. I haven't a clue which way the wind is blowing me nor how hard. As I said, the Canadian Arctic winds aloft can be ferocious. On the other hand, I do know a few things for sure: I'm somewhere above the Arctic Circlec my airspeed is 165 miles per hour, and I'm at 9,000 feet. Well, I also know two other things: I have no radio communication with anyone, and I have no navigation system other than a wandering magnetic compass, which, as I get closer to the Magnetic Pole, operates with a steadily diminishing sensitivity. Logic, but without first-hand experience, might suggest that the Pole's directional forces would increase with proximity. This wandering-about business is my first hint of what the compass needle will do directly over the Pole. I'm thinking now that the directionality will completely poop out before I get there. But, at this point, that's only a guess. And it's more than disconcerting.

Thirty minutes ago I should have picked up the radio beacon from Shepard Bay off to the left. But there was nothing. I wasted too much time looking for something to eat this morning and forgot to ask about my radio's failure to pick up the Baker Lake beacon earlier. Besides, you up there were supposed to remind me. Where were you when I needed you? Without thinking, I compromised navigation for appetite. Not smart. To make it worse, lunch at Baker Lake turned out to be the same as breakfast in Churchill, cheese-crackers and a Coke from the ice-free cooler.

The hours drone on. The disquiet of where I am and where I'm going grows exponentially. Apprehension changes its shape from the regular forms of logic to amorphous clouds of foreboding.

Clearly it's decision time. I am flying at 165 mph into a serious situation. But, as a matter of principle, I can't pull the plug. So I set a time limit on how long I will keep going. I decide to give it another 30 minutes. At that point, I will have flown 250 miles in the blind and without sun shots or radio contact with anyone. If the flight course has not been in the right direction, it is problematic. If the ADF radio is not receiving, this too is problematic. I would be far better off if I knew for sure that the radio was NOT working. Then I could just ignore it. But I also do know another thing for sure; the magnetic compass isn't at all trustworthy. The Pilot was right. It is useless.

I make a declaration to myself. If I have neither the sun nor a radio response at the next thirty-minute mark, I resolve to make a 180-degree turn and hope to get out of the clouds somewhere near where I flew into them. I write down the starting time, 1515 local. The sweep of the second hand is pointed straight up at the numeral twelve. I keep thinking, the sunshine I need might be just two minutes ahead.

In thirty minutes, I should still have enough fuel left to fly back to Baker Lake. Theoretically this will be another two hours. But if I have had a tailwind so far, it won't work. I will have gone too far into the clouds to make it back. Obviously, returning into a head wind will give me a net loss. But if I've had a head wind so far and I break out into sunshine, I should have nearly an hour of fuel left to figure out what to do next.

Now, dear reader, if you are still up there in your Critic's Loft looking down, you should have plenty of ideas to help me out. The problem is I can't hear you. I can only hear the engine and the arguing voices in my head. So I will continue along without your help. Thanks anyway.

The idea of ditching on the tundra without any notion of where I am is troubling, to say the least. If I can plan the landing with the engine still running, I know I will l survive my arrival. That is just pilotage. With engine power, you can hold the nose up and slow the plane way down. By hanging on the prop and dragging the tail, we can fly below stall speed and set down in ground effect. Dead stick landings without engine power are far more difficult. Having glider experience helps because all glider landings are without power. The big difference is that gliders have spoilers built into their wings; the spoilers act as brakes by killing your lift to get you down quickly when you need it. Dead-sticking a powered plane with no power is tough because you can't make any last-minute speed changes. Above all else, I keep telling myself, if I have not found an airport, for greater safety, I need to keep five minutes of fuel for the safest ditching.

Since we have thirty minutes to wait, I'll tell you a quick aside.

When I was flying back home from an afternoon of soaring a couple years ago, I took this Mooney up to 12,000 feet and cut the engine to see how well it would glide. The idea was to see how long I could keep it aloft. There were no thermals, so it didn't perform all that well. I kept changing airspeeds looking for the perfect one, but I couldn't get a definitive answer. I think somewhere around 85 miles per hour gave the slowest rate of descent.

The most curious thing is that once you cut the engine ignition, it's very hard to get the prop to stop windmilling. You have to pull the nose way up, almost to a stall before it quits rotating. Likewise it's hard to get the prop to kick over and restart with just airspeed alone. I had to push the nose over to accelerate the airplane to 155 miles per hour to get it to bump-start.

Now, back to work.

The 30-minute time-limit I gave myself is not a perfect solution. But it is a decision. The only alternative is to press on and hope Resolute pops into view.

I opt to chicken out. It is a decision in which I take little pride.

Just a few minutes into the 30-minute time window, the left fuel tank runs dry. The engine sputters. I switch to the right tank. She fires right back up. Half of my gas is now gone, but at least I have a reliable fuel gauge for the last half of my fuel supply. The air is thin. I feels as if the prolonged lack of oxygen has accelerated my heart rate. But maybe it's just pucker factor. Time is moving like you're under the hood on execution day, waiting for the electric jolt. Every tick of the second hand convinces me that I am flying farther away from logic and deeper into forlorn hope. What really bothers me is that I don't even know if I'm lost or not. If I hold my course and don't turn around, and if the winds are favorable and I break out of the clouds, I could wind up close to Resolute with an hour's fuel left just as I had planned. That thought keeps recycling in my brain.

I keep thinking that's the way things are supposed to work out. Besides, in the grand scheme of things, I have always been favored with good luck.

On the other hand, if the compass is wandering or the winds are errant, or if I can find no breaks in the overcast, there is no choice but to make a radio distress call on the emergency frequency. My only hope will be that somebody will hear it, and that I can find a place to land in what I hope is tundra below me. Right now I have no idea what the terrain looks like down there. I expect it's snow-covered Arctic marsh. But, for all I know, it could be the Arctic Ocean. As I said, Resolute Bay is a town on an island in the Canadian Archipelago. With a 70-knot tailwind, I could have already overshot it and be out over the Arctic Ocean. Of course I have no life raft. Oddly enough, I had worried about not having one when I crossed over Lake Michigan only the day before yesterday.

There's an old saying: "The Road of Life is paved with flattened squirrels who couldn't make a decision."

Either way, my decision is to not make any new decisions. Right or wrong, I'm sticking with my 30-minute deadline.

I keep looking at my watch. I can't resist it. When I'm not looking at it, I look at the panel clock. Right now, everything in my life is about the passage of time. I keep flying on. I search for the rationality in my decision-making. It has to be in there somewhere. With one's mind jumping all around, it's just hard to put your finger on anything.

The knot in my stomach might be hunger, but it could very well be something else.

The second hand finally ticks up to the twelve at the end of the last second of the last of minute. For some reason, it's important that I do not cheat by a single tick. As I'm making a standard rate turn, I try to make a radio call to Resolute one more time. Then I call on the emergency frequency, 121.5 mhz.

"Mayday, Mayday, Mayday." No answer. Nothing.

I call again in the blind, "Mayday, Mayday, Mayday. This is November, one, nine, two, eight Yankee, estimate 300 miles, ten degree radial north of Baker Lake at 9,000, flight planned for Resolute Bay, changing course to one nine zero, bound for Baker Lake. One soul on board. Two hours' fuel."

Of course I don't know if I'm headed for Baker Lake or not. All I want is to get out of the clouds so that I can take a sun shot. The information I gave will only tell whoever comes looking for me that I have turned back from Resolute. Nobody answered. The likelihood, of course, is that nobody heard my call.

The "estimate 300 miles north of Baker Lake," was a wild-ass guess. I can see neither sky nor earth. In the complete grayness that surrounds me, there is only one speck of color, the red gear-up warning light on the panel. Before I land and as the gear goes down, the red light blinks out and the green one next to it lights up. It's a little something to look forward to. If I land in the tundra, I will not lower the gear. We'll belly in.

As I dip the left wing to start the turn, I feel a rush of both regret and relief. I know I have at least another 250 miles of instrument flying ahead of me. Where on earth I will finally pop out of the clouds is completely up for grabs. If I do find sunlight to take a sun shot, I will have flown 500 miles blind on an uncertain compass. I've got to keep rejecting the idea that I've gotten myself into the ultimate crack.

I can feel that my rationality is becoming blunted even as my emotions are being sharpened

Is this experience of isolation and imminent peril the reason one pushes oneself beyond the bounds of good judgment? Is this the test we both fear and crave?

The answer to this question is at once equally obscure and self-evident.

Self-evident, because the need for individual validation is written all over it. Obviously, this is not a very encouraging assessment. Later, when I type my notes in the safety and comfort of my office, I'll know what you're thinking

Obscure, because there is so much more at work here than ego. There could be a dark side to it that requires more probing than is likely to happen here in this lonely, sealed capsule hurtling through space at 165 miles an hour.

Let me digress here for a moment. Most, but not all, of these emotional notions are noted in my journal. The emotions expressed therein are as real as the practical concern I have for saving my ass. As you know, in moments of eminent peril, there is little meaningful difference between the real and the imagined.

Now, even though I have turned back, the risk factor in my situation has not materially lessened. The wilderness to the south is every bit as dangerous as it is to the north, and maybe even more so. I've swapped the hope of picking up a radio signal from Resolute to the north for the hope of a good sun shot to the south. It could well be that I passed the point of no return half an hour ago. I won't know that for several more hours.

This is a good time for another aside. But my mind is blank. Well, actually it's not blank. It is chock-full of worry, and for now all asides are aside.

Finally, we emerge from the seemingly endless cloud bank. Glimpses of green-brown tundra appear through the scattered clouds below. I was wrong about the snow cover.

Finding the sun is clearly welcome news. (and *that* is an understatement!)

If I must make a forced landing up here, I have a rifle, a case of MREs (Meal Ready to Eat), Cokes, crackers and survival gear to last at least a couple of weeks. And, with a little luck, I'll have a few gallons of gas in the right wing tank to start a smoke-fire for a rescue beacon. I am still on an Instrument Flight Plan, and I have an Emergency Locator Transmitter. Of course I cannot even guess my latitude and longitude. But maybe I can calculate longitude by substituting the magnetic compass "north," and then reversing the formula. It would be terribly imperfect but hugely better than nothing. At best I would have an east-west coordinate. It takes an additional north-south coordinate to create a fixed point.

The chance of hiking to civilization is nil.

I see some lakes that roughly match up with the terrain shown on my chart. This suggests that I am about 175 miles east of where I should have been had there been no wind and my flying an accurate track. Man, I am way off course! If this is true, the wind is quite strong out of the northwest. This puts me a little closer to Churchill than Baker Lake. And the tailwind favors Churchill.

The next decision is easy. *Churchill, here I come.* Even so, it's going to be very close fuel-wise. To conserve gas, I throttle the engine back to 50 percent power. At this setting my airspeed will drop to about 125 miles per hour, and the added push from the quartering tailwind will give me a ground speed of around 150 mph.

But think about this. Some years ago, I had calculated that the airspeed with the best glide-ratio for my Mooney is about 85 miles per hour. If that airspeed maximizes my range, then it also makes sense that it should be my maintained airspeed.

I throttle back to 90 miles per hour. I figure this is within the margin of error.

As much as I try to settle down, my brain is constantly barraged with herky-jerky notions. For instance, I have to make a decision on which heading to take. My first thought is to head for the shoreline. That might lead me to where the likelihood of rescue is improved. There are settlements on the coast line. But that makes landing at Churchill less likely. Then, my brain switches to another solution. I'll switch to a direct bearing to Churchill and forget the shore line security. Then I'll think it through again and go back to the first heading. Fatigue, poor nutrition choices, emotional tension and oxygen deprivation combine to make a risky cocktail.

The only certainty I cling to is that if I run out of fuel before reaching Churchill, I will survive. As weird as this idea may sound, there is considerable comfort to it. The other appealing aspect of a forced, off-airport landing is that everything around me would stop — the wind, the engine noise, the drizzle running up the windscreen, the clouds, and the anxiety of not knowing which way is north; everything would stop. I would climb out of the plane. I would get out my gun, my food, my sleeping bag and most importantly, my emergency radio beacon. Everything would remain ghostly quiet until a helicopter would wop, wop, wop in and rescue me. Sure, this is crazy thinking. But, what the heck? It feels reassuring, and that feels good.

Back to serious. The only unknown now is where the next landing will be. I'm pulling hard for that beautiful, long runway at Churchill International. I make a final decision to compromise the perceived safety of the shore line and stick with the shorter, direct approach. I wish now I had checked Churchill's forecast weather at Baker Lake. But who the hell thought I'd end up there today?

Finally, after another twenty minutes of calculating and recalculating, comes the first really good news since exiting that huge Arctic cloud mass. Emerging up under the nose is a big blue body of shallow water, the Hudson Bay. I match the shore contours with a chart and determine that I'm about 200 miles north of Churchill. Because I am all throttled back, call it two hours. My fuel consumption is way down, so it might just all work out. If I'm right about the quartering tailwind out of the northwest, that could reduce the time to, say, 90 minutes. But the unknown wind speed and the engine's lessened fuel consumption make accurate calculations impossible. Any way you look at it, there is zero reserve with respect to fuel.

More importantly, there really is no alternative. I start a gentle climb to 13,000 feet in hopes of picking up some more tailwind. Then I throttle back even more to save as much fuel as I can. I lean the mixture control until the engine starts to sputter, then twist the knob gently until it barely fires evenly on all four cylinders. With a tailwind and reduced fuel consumption, I give Mother Nature more time to help us along. These are free miles, but I'm only slicing minutes here, maybe only seconds. Keep in mind that we're cruising at less than two miles a minute. But the time difference between landing a half- minute short of the airport and landing with a half a minute of fuel left in the tanks is only 60 seconds. That minute might save a mile and a half of expensive embarrassment.

Fifty miles north of Churchill, I call Approach Control. The undercast flows from the landmass before evaporating out over the bay. Tower calls back and clears me for an instrument approach.

This would be great news, except that I don't have an instrument approach plate for Churchill. While I'm scurrying to gather all the information I can from miscellaneous charts, I hear a plane on frequency advising Churchill Tower of a "Missed Approach." This is not good news. It probably means that the other plane came down to 200 feet—the minimum altitude for an instrument approach—and couldn't see the runway. The pilot then declared a "Missed Approach." The tower asked his intentions and he requested a "Go Around." They want to shoot a second approach. That part of the transmission is encouraging. It says they're still in the game and probably feel that they can do a little better this time. So I am in the game too. I start drawing my own approach plate. It will be as striped down as I can make it: headings, altitudes, and tower radio frequencies. I admit that the rare air and anxiety of the last six or seven hours is taking their toll on my ability to keep a clear head. But there is comfort in the fact that, one way or the other, all of this apprehension will come to a conclusion within the next 20 minutes.

For some reason, my sense of urgency doesn't heighten. I slow the plane down even more but hold on to my precious altitude. When I'm about 15 miles out, I still cannot see the airport. It and the surrounding landmass remain beneath the undercast. The other plane is shooting its second approach. I keep sketching on my handmade approach plate.

Come on, baby, I urge the other plane. *Squeeze!*

In about two minutes, Churchill tower tells the other plane to switch to Ground Control. They landed! That means that they either busted minimums, or the airport's not totally socked in. If they made it, I know damn good and well that I'll make it. But I'm running on fumes and I'll make it on my first try. I have no choice.

I swing into the approach pattern and Tower clears me to land. I line up on the glideslope and descend down into the clouds — my old friend, the clouds.

The left tank ran dry two and one-half hours ago, and the right tank fuel gauge needle has stopped bumping off the E. It's pegged. This means the float sensor is sitting on the bottom of a near-empty tank. I center the plane up on the invisible runway using the localizer needle on the instrument panel. Altitude is the only thing I have in good supply. Altitude is like both time and energy in the bank. I hate like hell to give any of it away.

There is something very interesting in a situation like this. Fear plays little or no part in the process. There is only concentration. Clear, sweet concentration. The brain clears itself of absolutely everything except the task right in front of you. Perfect mental cleansing. There is nothing else like it in the world. You gotta love it!

Although my instrument needles are centered for both the glideslope and the localizer, my airspeed is too high, and pushing the nose down for the approach is making it worse. The airspeed indicator now reads 130 miles per hour. That's twice too fast to land, or even to lower my flaps and landing gear. I'd been too unwilling to give away altitude earlier, having become convinced that I'd have great need of it if my fuel ran out short of the airport. Now, in hindsight, I realize I should have set up the approach to let the plane fly itself in like this was an everyday landing. I break out of the clouds at 400 feet above the ground and I'm already a third of the way down the runway. Visibility goes from zero to five miles just like that. But I'm both high and hot. I pull the throttle back to idle-cutoff. Down goes the landing gear, even above maximum gear extension speed. I pitch the plane sideways into a steep, wing-down, sideslip. Speed bleeds off fast when you're going sideways. I pump in full flaps (also above max flap speed) and increase the slip even further. In the corner of my eye I see the town of Churchill off to the left and the Hudson Bay spreading off to the right just like I left it. The landing morphs from being a little frantic into a firm implant followed by some determined braking. I stop with a full hundred yards of runway to spare.

Piece of cake.

There is no final gasp of relief or urge to kiss the ground. All my emotional wiring is still plugged into the concentration mode. I will mentally re-play this approach many times in the future. It really was lovely how it turned out.

I will also wonder if I didn't subconsciously feel that by successfully returning to safety, I got cheated out of an entirely different adventure. Think about that one, up there, will you?

I taxi to the tower to close my Flight Plan. They don't ask about the Mayday call I had sent out a couple of hours ago. Apparently no one received it. I don't really want to talk about it, so I didn't ask. That's all behind me now.

Naturally I then taxi over to The Pilot's C-46 hangar. The big doors are closed and there's no sign of life. In a way I'm disappointed. But in another way I'm just fine being by myself. To tell the truth, I carry a measure of shame I don't wish to share right now.

Face to face with uncertainty, serious though it was, I turned back.

I really need to spool down alone.

That I was here only twelve hours ago seems impossible. It feels like it's been two lifetimes. I park the Mooney in what is now my favorite sheltered spot on the apron, sit on the wing and listen to the wind blowing through the great, grey metal hangars. To my engine noise-numbed ears, the doors still rattle in random metallic rhythms. The music is still sadder than all hell. It's a dirge, a rattling requiem.

Remembering again that Churchill's dry, I shift a couple of Buds from the cooler to my bag before I tie down and lock up my soul mate. Then I thumb a ride to town and reregister at the Arctic Inn.

Penny, the smiling, plumpish and friendly proprietress, is happy to see me back, and she invites me to share a dinner of Arctic char with her and several friends there at the motel. I can see their dinner table right behind the counter. The welcome smell of cooked vegetables drifts over to the small lobby area. It is a gracious invitation that's offered in the friendliest and most inviting manner. But I have to decline. I'm still wound up inside; I'm not ready for people. I also don't feel like I deserve her kindness, or anyone else's kindness for that matter. I am still too ashamed for having turned back.

A block away, I find a modest restaurant and eat char by myself. No one else is eating there. So now I sit in my puddle of self-pity wishing like hell that I had accepted Penny's invitation. But, in reality, I'm still way too far out of sync for social engagement. I can think of nothing in the world I want to talk about with anyone. So I talk to myself, in my head, and it's disconsolation in its finest form.

Just to prove my disappointment with myself, I don't call home. I really don't want to come up with either explanations or excuses. Sharing anything now is intolerable. I'll worry about how to exonerate myself when I get back to Atlanta.

The motel room is the same as it was last night. It still stinks of other people's habits. And tonight it offers the same fitful and interrupted tossing.

Eventually I get up and thumb another ride back out to the airport. The weather this morning is rotten all over Canada. There are no thunderstorms, but everything is solid overcast, poor visibility and rain. The monstrous Arctic low I had tried to penetrate yesterday now dominates the whole tenderloin of the northern part of the Continent.

At the airport I finagle some recently out-of-date Instrument Approach Plates for some key airports to the south. The generosity comes from two middle-aged pilots patiently waiting at the weather station for better weather. They're flying a twin engine Cessna. They are both very friendly and seem to have no problem waiting for the weather to get above their *personal minimums.* Apparently those limits are more strict than the ones posted on the Approach Plates. Still, there is something compelling about their attitude toward the challenges of flying. They both seem happy and easy-going, as if they are in a partnership with natural phenomena. They appear to actually enjoy sitting around the terminal talking to people.

I try to relax and tell them I'm up here just to do some sight-seeing. I mention nothing of yesterday's failure. The interesting thing, to my mind at least, is how you might view these two fellows. You, up there, have just gone through all that flying in the soup, the about-to-run-out-of-gas thing and then just barely making it back to Churchill. But these guys are on an entirely different wavelength. Stretching boundaries is not their thing.

Perhaps they are made of a finer fabric. Their interest is in planning a trip and then thoroughly refining its execution. Man, I admire that. The expression that comes to mind is, "I'd give anything for that quality." But, for me, that's not entirely true. Still, I'd give a lot for just some of that quality. These gentlemen carry their maturity well. Maybe I've still got some time to learn.

If I saw The Pilot as a Sage, then these two old pilots are akin to Oracles. They turned up only with the purpose to show me the other side of an approach to adventure. If I'm right, Churchill might be full of Prophets. Maybe it really is a Church Hill. And wouldn't it be neat if all the Oracles hung out at the airport?

But, no matter. I'm really impressed but I'm not a convert yet. My immediate mindset is definitely not to hang around here any longer than I have to. No matter what the meteorological conditions, I'm going to take it on. I'm still the old me.

The weather south, all the way to the Great Lakes, is definitely rotten. So rather than going due south through the worst of it, I'll head west to fly with the counter-clockwise flow of the low pressure system. This way I stay out of the worst of it and maybe catch a little tailwind.

See? I'm learning already.

Enough of that. I file an Instrument Flight Plan, strap on the Mooney, and I'm back in the soup.

The first stop is Thompson, Manitoba. It feels like a remote post. A fast turnaround, a quick download of junk food, and I head to International Falls, Minnesota. The first leg takes two hours, and the second takes four. Both are on solid instruments all the way. There's no sightseeing. I can't tell you a thing about the endless Canadian wilderness. It is only me, the artificial horizon directly in front of my nose, and the noisy drone of the steady old Lycoming up front doing its thing.

An hour in International Falls nets me two microwaved hot dogs (finally a good meal), a Coke, an easy customs inspection, a weather briefing, and both wing tanks full of avgas. Flying now with only one fuel gauge feels perfectly normal. Out of International Falls, I climb through the overcast to 9,000 feet where there is brilliant sun and bright blue sky looking down on the solid, pillowy-white under-cast below. The Earthlings down there in America are having light rain. I say, *let 'em get wet.* I should have shaken it by now, but I'm still isolated. It gives me some time to think a little more about the two wiser pilots I left in Churchill. Why was I so disconnected with everything around me while they were so totally engaged?

Maybe the longer one indulges in loneliness, the more one needs it. And the more one needs it, the more the responsibility of returning to Earth feels like a chore. The buying of fuel, meeting people, talking to meteorologists and filing Flight Plans become annoying invasions of my inward-looking solitude. Even choosing which cold, ready-made, vending-machine sandwich to eat is a personal intrusion. I wonder if lonely isn't just another wonderful addiction: you hate it, but you need more of it. And you know it's bad for you. But you're afraid you are going to run out it. Then what do you do?

It is now 600 miles later and ten o'clock at night. It's pitch dark, and I'm cleared for the approach into Champaign, Illinois. My eyes are so tired that after every blink, I get a watery blur. I wipe them clear, and then I try not to blink again. Because I can no longer read the small print on the charts, I have to ask

Approach Control for the radio frequency for the tower. This is embarrassingly unprofessional.

Lining up with the runway lights, for me, makes a night landing easier than day landings. At three miles out, the runway lights are just two parallel dotted lines. As you get closer the perspective widens at the near end, and then you fly into an inverted vee. You just throttle back and aim right at the threshold, and everything just works itself out swimmingly. Even when you're exhausted, you just got to love them.

Once refueled and the weather checked to Atlanta, I make my first inspired move of the day. I call home to announce a post-midnight arrival.

Nancy answers cheerfully. I try to disguise it, but fatigue and not talking much all day makes my voice gravely.

In a stumbling way, I start to explain the whole failed North Pole mission. That was just yesterday, but it feels so long ago. It's hard to make much sense at all. But before I'm a minute into it, she interrupts.

"Richard, you sound terrible. Find a motel and go have a nice meal. Everything's fine here, so take your time. We'll have a special dinner waiting for you tomorrow night. Everybody here misses you." I'd like to think that really includes everybody, but you'd never ask about things like that. Nobody would.

I'm really not a weeping-willow type. However, sometimes, dog-tired and emotionally spent, one can be forgiven just about anything. Right?

In the darkened evening at the airport here in Champaign, I sit alone on the sturdy wing of my faithful friend. In one more hop, this brief journey will have covered a distance equal to a fourth of the circumference of Earth. It is now winding down with a conspicuously lonely dinner of a Snickers bar and the last two beers from a foam cooler that hasn't seen an ice cube in three days.

I'm not home yet, but I'm already looking at this little episode in retrospect. Right now, none of these last few days feel the least bit like an adventure. Instead, they feel like disappointment overlaid with fatigue, humility, and hunger. It's all wrapped up in one expensive, unsatisfying package called failure. And, of course, the obvious question is, should I have kept on going to the Pole and not turned back? Had I made it, the trip would have stirred the hearts of every reader of this journal. But since I turned back in the face of uncertainty, it surely must be called something less than inspiring. Maybe it's just a misadventure. Whatever you choose to call it, I think you will agree that it really sucks.

Obviously that's an unproductive train of thought, so I turn my thinking to something more immediate: I'd give anything for some cheese and crackers to go with this warm beer and this candy bar with its wrapper glued to it. But the crackers are long gone, and now the airport is closed and locked up.

So I start hoofing it.

After a mile's walk down an unlit country highway flanked with sweet-smelling, ten-foot-tall cornfields, I find a third class motel and check in. I have to wake up the guy running the place. My night is restless. I'm way too wired and exhausted to sleep. All night I lie waiting for the sun to come up.

Of course it does, and the next morning's flight to Atlanta is as boring as a commercial red-eye. I just sit in the cockpit and watch the clouds go by. There is neither the joy of flying nor any sense of peril. Being cleared for the approach to Peachtree Airport doesn't even feel like coming home. The return to the routines of everyday life hasn't sunk in yet.

I'm still an outsider.

Right now, the main thing on my mind remains the disappointment of this last week. From your perch way up there, it must look like there's not much to show for this second effort. And you may be right.

Then, taxiing in, I see the whole world change one more time. All of the glass in the Epps terminal has been installed since I left a week ago. Man, it looks good! The glass successfully accentuates the curved, structural, wooden arches. Pat's brother, Ben, hand-built these piece by piece in one of PDK's WWII-era asbestos-board buildings. The trusses mimic the structure of the wooden ribs in the wings of Howard Hughes' giant Spruce Goose seaplane. But the entire expressive form of the building has finally taken shape. It is well composed, bold and innovative. And it successfully fulfills the dream of its architect.

And there is no feeling in the world that can match that!

This year's North Pole disappointment recedes quickly, or at least it hides in a far, dark corner of my mind. I tell myself I did the best I could, and that's the best I can do. There is always next year.

Parenthetically, a week after getting back home, I asked the avionics department at Epps Aviation to check out the ADF, the radio that didn't do its job and I forgot to check twice in Canada. They determined that the radio would not receive 60 percent of its bandwidth. The frequencies lost included both of the stations I needed to finish my mission. Most notably, the radio could not have picked up the Resolute Bay radio beacon. This blind spot in the ADF's receiving spectrum could have turned me into "Polar

Bear take-out," as my friend George Cully so cleverly couched it. What is really curious about this is that I still feel no less guilty about making the decision to turn around.

But, as the great polar explorer and adventurer Norman D. Vaughan once said, "You haven't failed until you quit." There will always next year.

CHAPTER 4

THE THIRD SHOT
AT THE POLE

August 10, 1980 — August 17, 1980

L AST YEAR'S FAILED attempt at the Pole will never be forgotten — at least not by me. It now resides as carefully typed notes next to the original, hand-scrawled legal pads and journals stashed away months ago in a file drawer in the back of my office. It's filed away right next to 1978's magnificent flop.

So far we're zero for two.

The new Epps Aviation Terminal, on the other hand, is a success in every respect. The terminal's customers love it. Pat, his wife Ann and the three kids all love it. And Pat's architects are as proud of it as Pat is. From the first napkin sketch to the final punch list, the whole process was a mixture of creativity and practicality. Successful architectural experiences are like lasting love affairs, except they have one huge advantage: the buildings don't get a vote.

The week I took off last year to go north imposed no negative impact on the construction process. Yes, I know. Go ahead and say it.

The new terminal sits at a commanding location on DeKalb Peachtree Airport. On the opposite corners of the largest hangar are the county airport offices and a local restaurant and bar called The Downwind. The *downwind leg* is a term used for the first leg in a standard approach pattern to any airport. It's followed by the *base leg* and then the *final approach*. After work, pilots tend to meet at The Downwind (the restaurant, not the pattern), to do what pilots do best: critique other pilots.

A couple of weeks ago, in July, Pat and I were practicing this ritual. Some think of it as earning Continuing Ed credits on your pilot's license, but the FAA has a different view on this. They require a regulations review and test flight every two years with one of their designees. Really gung-ho pilots follow both procedures.

But, back to The Downwind.

"Ok, so you almost run out of gas and the radio's not working. You don't know where you are, and you're in the clouds, right? The engine's still running, so why'd you turn back? You're supposed to keep going." This is Epps talking. After half a glass of juice (Epps' term for house wine), he automatically reverts to the present tense. This is Pat's way to shift into his "story-telling mode." All his tales are spun in the present tense. Past tense is what old men and has-beens use.

I try not to be defensive. "Of course there's no way to know for sure, but if I had not turned around, I believe I'd still be up there somewhere, wandering all over the tundra looking for Resolute."

"Well, maybe. Show me dat sun compass trick again. I wanna figure it out." The shift of "that" to "dat" is further indication of story-mode transference. Pat was born and raised in Athens, Georgia, so maybe it's a Southern culture thing.

On a paper napkin I write down the local time in 24-hour form. I start the narrative, "Then add four hours to convert it to Greenwich Mean Time. Then multiply that number by 15."

Epps takes my felt tip and circles the 15. "Now where did you get this number?"

I answer, "Simple. You take the 360 degrees the earth turns in a day and divide that by 24 hours."

Pat picks it up, "So, 15 is the number of degrees the sun travels in an hour. If you subtract the time since the sun was aligned with the Prime Meridian at Greenwich noon and move it by the elapsed time, which will point you to the sun. That makes sense. Take the reciprocal of that number, and you have its shadow. Pretty clever!"

Epps's backcountry syntax aside, he's really smarter'n hell. His mechanical engineering degree from Georgia Tech doesn't hurt either.

We go outside on the observation deck that overlooks the runways to test the numbers in the evening sun. It works just as it's supposed to. After setting the shadow on the calculated number, the hand-drawn compass card is oriented to True North. Its accuracy is verified by approximating true north from runway 34 right in front of us. You do remember that runway numbers are magnetic, don't you?

Pat is really getting into this thing. It's like teaching a kid to juggle. Once he gets the knack, he wants to keep doing it. But it's July, so we go back inside where it's air-conditioned.

He sits and sips a minute while I start to recount the peril of last year's endeavor. I'm just getting my rhythm, and of course, he's not listening. Then, out of the blue, "I think I know where I can get a 15-gallon reserve tank. We mount it in the back seat of Seven Six Romeo. We plug in a back- up ADF radio, and we're good to go, heh? Besides my Bonanza is aerobatic and your Mooney's not. So we take it. Whatcha think?"

"Hell, I'm ready. When do we leave?"

"I'm thinkin' two weeks, maybe the tenth." This is in August.

I answer, "Done deal. I'll start pulling together survival equipment tomorrow. We'll find us a tent, some sleeping bags, a gun, ammo, food, and some cold weather gear!"

"A gun? Whatcha gonna do, fire a salute over the Pole?"

Those thousands of lonely square miles of forest that turn into lonely square miles of tundra at the tree line are still vivid in my mind. There are grizzly bears in those woods, and there are polar bears on that tundra.

I simplify the issue, "Remember the old joke about why men have nipples? The gun is 'just in case'."

Epps smiles. "We're on our way."

This is classic Epps. On the surface it looks like instant decision-making. When you get to know him better, though, you know that he had rolled this thing around in his head and worked out most of the wrinkles weeks ago.

Since going north by myself last year, I've had plenty of time to think about the downside of an emergency landing in the Arctic. On that flight, I took a light sleeping bag, a cooler of junk food, some Cokes, a six-pack of beer, and a thousand dollars in greenbacks. That was several factors more preparation than the previous year. But still it was only in the *token effort* category. This year will be different. This year we're going to be prepared.

Going back up there with Epps will obviously change the dynamics significantly. We've been pretty good friends for 15 years, and even though we are two entirely different personality types, we seem to amplify one another's fundamental abilities in a positive way. Pat's an extrovert; gregarious and comfortable with people. I'm not so much that way. That said, neither of us is extreme in this snapshot portrayal. Sometimes he will turn inward and withdraw, and sometimes I can be open and friendly. Overriding these differences is a mutual compatibility and trust that makes each of us a stronger person. When we have differing opinions on things, it simply doesn't seem to make much difference. And even then, the differences are almost never obstacles. What I'm trying to describe here is the time-honored essence of all true friendships.

Just before dawn on the 10th, I kiss Nancy, our one-year old son Richard and Lee, our five-year old daughter, goodbye. The kids are still tucked in bed asleep. In keeping with tradition, Nancy says, "Remember your responsibilities. If you need help, call." She still never adds, "Be careful."

Pat also arrives at the airport alone; Ann and his three kids remain at home. I assume he has just been through a similar drill. It's one of those age-old moments that go back as far as Papa Neanderthal leaving the cave in hunt of a mammoth herd. You just leave the cave with Mama Neanderthal and go do it. (And, no, not for a moment do I think I won't hear about that.)

We load the survival equipment: a 20-gauge Remington and a case of MREs. We also have a cooler full of junk food, a six-pack of beer, winter jackets, two winter sleeping bags and a four-man tent. With the gear loaded, we each put $3,000 in cash in one money belt." Epps says to me, "You da bank."

Pat's plane is a single engine, four-seat Bonanza that has been beefed-up to perform aerobatics. It has a little shorter fuselage than Zip's Bonanza we took the first time. As you'll remember, Pat flies his plane in air shows around the country. It performs as beautifully and gracefully as flying gets this side of a bald eagle. In fact, a bald eagle can only dream he could do an inverted snap-roll like Pat.

Last week Pat had his maintenance mechanics install the 15-gallon reserve gas tank in the passenger seat location behind the pilot. It sits on a rack, and all you have to do is reach around, open a valve, and voila! You have another 75 minutes' fuel gravity-feeding into the left wing-tank. That will be our emergency reserve. Our plan is to **not** use this fuel except in a real emergency. But in practice, we will use it on most of the 13 long flights we will make in the next week.

We've almost finished loading the plane when Epps hauls in a mounted main-landing gear wheel. He must have found it in the corner of a hangar or something. He then adds an inflatable life raft and two life jackets. This seems strange, since there are only the Great lakes and the Hudson Bay between Atlanta and the Pole. Sometimes I have to wonder what he's thinking. Nonetheless, with a measure of pride, we look at our conspicuous efforts for personal safety. The survival gear makes us feel almost like explorers, and that this is almost an expedition.

It's 7:15 am. The sun is up, and the sky is filled with scattered clouds. Pat cranks up the Bonanza, taxis out to Runway 20 Left, pours on the coals, and we're off. Our first destination is Thunder Bay, Canada; it takes us six non-stop hours to complete that 850-mile leg. There's a stiff headwind enroute, so we have to use the fuel in the emergency tank. But, man, does this added range help the program. Last year I had to stop twice for fuel.

I file a Request for Customs, but unlike last year, I don't inadvertently cancel it. Legal entry is a breeze when you do it right. This is now my fifth trip into Thunder Bay.

We land there, gas up, eat a vending machine sandwich and listen to the Flight Service guys expand on why all the radios and compasses will be permanently damaged by flying to the Magnetic Pole. This is our third attempt, and the authoritative admonitions have not decreased. It's only midafternoon, so we hop back in the plane and keep going. This is my leg. It's 760 miles to Churchill. Remember, they're halfway up the western shore of the Hudson Bay. On the approach to their airport, we look for both polar bears on the land side and white whales in the Bay. Just like last year, we spot neither.

But we've been haulin' the mail! Today we've flown 1,600 miles. Except for the headwind, the weather was unchallenging, and the plane purred the whole way. The only thing really happening is totally subjective. It has to do with the mental transformation that comes with being separated from the responsibilities of work-a-day life. Almost as soon as we take off, that separation begins. The mind loosens the ties to all those connections ranging from economic and professional obligations to family commitments and responsibilities. None of those connections is severed. Instead, let's just say that they're re-prioritized.

The cloud cover enroute is scattered to broken. I off-set our course, and we come up on Churchill 15 miles off to our left, just like we're supposed to. The landing is routine and we taxi around the big gray hangars looking for my old mentor. There is no sign of either The Pilot or his big transport.

I call into town to ask that they send out a cab. Penny is not at the Arctic Inn to renew her dinner invitation from last year, but we find a substantial meal in a restaurant around the corner. Flopping down in our hotel room after an adequate repast feels pretty damn good. When we turn in, our ears are still drumming, and the adrenalin is still flowing. The sun, on the other hand, is showing no signs of resting. The whole world is still in a go-mode, and Epps and I are on a roll. Atlanta to Churchill in one day, WOW!

Back at the airport the next morning, we look around again for The Pilot. I want Epps to meet him, but he's still nowhere to be found. We're airborne at 10:20 a.m. and I fly the 750 miles to Cambridge Bay. Again, the extra tank in the back seat makes a huge difference. We're now 200 miles north of the Arctic Circle and this is about as far as I got last year. The weather is beautiful, mostly scattered clouds with plenty of sunshine. The GMT-times-15 sun shots are easy, and we shoot one every 20 minutes. Epps can't get enough of them.

The terrain below us is uniform scrub vegetation growing out of brown tundra and pockmarked with lakes and rivulets as far as we can see in every direction. There is no evidence of ice or snow. In the winter, this will be a uniformly white wasteland and readily navigable by foot, dog sled or snowmobile. In the summer, because the terrain is sodden, much of the population up here is geographically isolated.

The paved strip at Cambridge Bay is a couple of miles from town, but they have a first class meteorological station at the airport. We're only 450 miles from Resolute Bay. Unfortunately, the forecast for that destination is zero/zero. That means zero-visibility and zero-ceiling, and "zero" is not good by any standard.

My thinking is that we have pressed very hard to get this far. Because of the disappointing forecast, maybe it's time take a little rest and plan this next leg more carefully. The Arctic has a well-earned reputation for being unforgiving of errors. I'm still recovering from the time I spent flying around blind in the clouds here last year.

This is Epps' leg to fly, and he's not in a sitting-around mode. We're walking to the plane when I suggest taking a little break to think this thing through. He doesn't slow his pace, "Hell, we'll just fly on up there, look around, maybe shoot an approach and if we don't like it, we'll just fly back here and spend the night. Come on. Lez go!"

We're talking about the distance from New York City to Cleveland, Ohio, and back with no form of human habitation in between.

So I default to the obvious, "Well, what about that zero/zero forecast?"

Unfazed, he says, "What do you mean? That's the good news. The weather never stays zero/zero very long. It can't. You know that. It's gonna be scattered to broken when we get there! You wait and see. Come on. Lez go!"

He hasn't slowed his pace. He's still strutting with his nose pointed directly at the airplane.

Epps in *lez go-mode* is logic-intolerant. But with the extra 15 gallons of fuel in the backseat tank, we should have enough gas to go there and back with maybe an hour's reserve. I have an uncomfortable feeling, but my case is not airtight. So I quit bellyaching. Besides, I tell myself, we have nothing else to do this afternoon. Might as well go flying.

We climb to 8,000 feet and drone on for several hours through sunshine and over scattered cumulus puff-clouds. Below us there's nothing but an endless landscape of brown and green tundra grass. It's my turn to do sun shots three times an hour. Then, just as I'm about to buy Pat's flim-flam argument that "bad weather only gets better," I look at the horizon ahead. A large cloud formation is building into what looks like an impenetrable black fortress. We're 25 miles from the barricade, and we can see that the formation goes from the ground to above the service ceiling of our little airplane. It's a bark-textured, rough-edged wall that extends from horizon to horizon. The good news is that we're only 65 miles from Resolute and locked 5x5 with both their radio transmitter and navigation beacons. Pat, the great communicator, likes to handle his own radio. He calls Resolute Approach for a weather check.

They answer, "Roger, November eight one seven six Romeo. Resolute weather: ceiling zero, visibility zero. No wind. Altimeter 28.94. Say your intentions. Over."

Pat answers, "Seven six Romeo, We're gonna shoot the approach. Over."

"Resolute Approach, we have a Twin Otter on the approach now. We'll keep you advised. Out."

They then give the deHavilland DHC-6 light transport some headings, and we monitor their progress with great attention. If they make it, we'll make it.

Upon penetrating the cloud bank, we find it surprisingly stable. We're flying on instruments alone, without visual reference to either the ground below or the sun above. But we're locked on to Resolute's radio beacons. I'm keeping track of our location with my finger moving slowly on the chart. The chart is spread out on my left leg where Pat can see both it and my locating finger.

He's good at this game and will probably not need all this. But it's there, "just in case."

Approach Control slows us down to 120 knots and gives us headings to line up about five miles behind the Twin Otter. This is good. We'll just follow them in. We're all ears as they start their final approach. They are in the same pea soup as we're in. We're urging them on. Again, if they can land, we can land.

Silent minutes go by. Pat and I are not talking. Then, in a matter-of-fact voice, we hear the Otter call, "Missed approach".

Tower asks their intentions, and they say that they are going to fly out to a navigation intersection "and hold for a little while." They don't have to say it, but we know what they actually intend. They're waiting to see what we are going to do. In aviation circles, the Twin Otter is affectionately known as a Twotter.

"Hold" means that they will fly a racetrack-shaped pattern with a pair of legs that are each one-minute long and joined by one-minute, 180-degree turns at both ends. The total time for one lap is four minutes. This is done with low power settings at a prescribed altitude, so they can wait comfortably for the weather to improve and use as little fuel as possible.

So now it's our turn. Approach Control gives us final headings to line up on the Localizer Beam about ten miles out from the airport. We swing left onto the beam and line up for the invisible runway. If we stay on the beam, we'll be correctly aligned in terms of left and right. We ease down to 2,500 feet. There is no visibility outside the plane. At two and one-half miles out, we intercept the glide slope radio beam and start our gradual descent down to the minimum allowable altitude: 200 feet above the ground. If we stay on the left and right bream (localizer) and the up and down beam (glide slope), we'll be aligned for the threshold of the runway. I have my forehead on the inside of the co-pilot window looking for anything that hints of Mother Earth. I keep my eyes always moving so that nothing is lost in my retinal blind spots.

Starting at 500 feet on the altimeter, I call out altitudes every 50 feet. Pat is focused on keeping the navigation needles centered. He's *the eye* for the instruments, but he still steals peeks outside. I am *the eye* for the outside. But I watch the altimeter and glide slope indicators, too. This is not a matter of distrusting the other guy. It's a matter of both of us knowing everything that's going on. We have equal money riding on the success of this approach. The airfield elevation is 15 feet above mean sea level. I call, "Two fifteen, MSL." Pat levels out and holds us precisely at 215 feet above mean sea level. That puts us at 200 feet above the runway. This is the published minimum permissible altitude for seeing the runway to land here. We fly straight and level for exactly one minute. There is not the first sign of terra firma below. We're flying through homogenized, 100 percent whole milk. Calmly, Pat calls the tower, "Missed Approach".

The Tower acknowledges and asks our intentions. I'm thinking, *Cambridge Bay, here we come.*

Epps is on the horn and there's no hesitation in his voice. "Seven six Romeo, request another approach."

I know what this means as sure as I know anything. I also know that there is not a damn thing in the world I can do about it either. We're going to land here at this airport. And if everything lines up as solidly as it did on this first approach, this time we will land. Pat is resolved. He doesn't need to spell it out.

The flying for this last approach was absolute precision. We knew exactly where we were with respect to the runway every moment. The altitudes were rock solid. Our minds were in complete accord.

There was been no hurrying and no uncertainty in this entire flight. Pat is in his element.

The tower gives us radar headings to work us around for our second approach.

"That was good," Pat says evenly. "We're going to do exactly the same thing again, but maybe go just a little bit lower." That's Epps-speak for *"land this baby on the runway".*

I cannot explain this logically, but my feelings about this second approach are totally opposite from the caution I felt upon leaving Cambridge Bay. The approach Epps just shot was one of the most precise instrument procedures I have ever experienced. There was no wind or turbulence. Pat is flying like a laser-guided autopilot and I am tracking our cross- coordinates on the chart like the winner of a national Etch A Sketch competition.

There is absolutely no confusion, no uncertainty, no urgency and no hesitation. I also know that if I raise my hand and call, "Abort!" Epps will firewall the throttle, pull back the controls and we'll climb out in a heartbeat. As I said, this is a high-stakes game. We are outside the envelope but in complete control. It's a feeling you never get in real life.

We line up the second time at exactly the same navigation intersection and repeat the drill. If Pat keeps both the horizontal localizer needle and the vertical glideslope needle pegged at their respective center points, with the wings remaining level and our airspeed just right, we will contact the center line of runway at just a few miles per hour above stall speed. If he's off, we'll call a missed approach and either go around for another try or abort altogether. We both check for the green lights confirming that our gear is down and that we're drawing fuel from the fullest tank. As opposed to calling the copilot for "flaps" as many pilots do, Pat and I each run our own. It gives you more of a feeling of control. We also each do our own landing gear retraction and extension. It's all part of a rhythm.

As we come down to minimums, I call out altitudes and subtract the 15 feet, "250 feet, 200 feet, 150 feet, 100 feet, no contact, slow it down, 50 feet, no contact, I'm all eyeballs, Klondike. Slow it down, ... 80 knots ... OK, I got a runway light ... off the wing tip, my side ... hold this heading ... hold it off ... hold if off!"

Kaboompf, rumble, rumble, rumble.

Epps brakes firmly but does not lock up the tires. We roll to a stop. The runway is gravel, so there is no painted centerline or edge markings. All we can see are two dim, glowing runway lights 30 feet away on my side of the plane. We have not a clue where we are with respect to buildings, taxiways or anything else at the airport.

We both exhale.

The Tower cannot see us, but they call, "Seven six Romeo, Resolute Tower, what is your situation?"

Epps answers, "Seven six Romeo, we're on the ground. Request taxi instructions."

I look over. You know that grin by now.

Hell, talk about having the most fun you can have with your clothes on!

The tower asks our position, and, of course we have no idea where we are. Pat responds, "Hold on a minute." He arbitrarily picks a direction in the fog, revs the engine and starts taxiing, very slowly. We come up on a low, red, wooden fence. He calls the tower, "Seven Six Romeo is off the south side of the runway and we're over here by the red wooden fence."

The tower answers, "Seven six Romeo, we have many wooden fences here, and they are all red. Hold your position until we can locate you."

"Seven six Romeo, roger that." A pilot is supposed to repeat a radio command to make sure it is fully understood. But the Boss Man is now in the catbird seat and gets a little slack. He shuts down the engine but leaves the radios on, and we sit here in comfortable silence. We're completely full of ourselves, but it is my buddy here who gets to put the O/O entry in his log book. A zero/zero landing on a gravel runway at the end of civilization takes a little time to fully digest.

Five minutes later, the Twin Otter calls in and asks about "the single engine plane's second approach." The Tower tells them we landed. The Otter asks for the ceiling for our landing. Pat picks up the mike and interrupts. "Seven Six Romeo, we found a break in the clouds right at the south end of the runway." The Otter pilot knows, the tower knows, and Pat knows that this is standard operating procedure for busting minimums. But the Otter still makes another approach. We hear him buzz through the soup, right down the runway, probably at 100 feet.

He calls, "Missed Approach," then heads back to his holding pattern.

After 20 minutes of our just sitting, the fog begins to lift. It doesn't thin out, but you can look under its skirt to see the bottom five or six feet of red buildings and fences a few hundred feet away. Pat cranks up the Bonanza, calls the tower, and we are cleared to taxi to a red Quonset hut that serves as the Resolute terminal.

Leaving the plane parked at the gas pumps, we walk on the gravel apron over to an adjacent Quonset hut. This is the Resolute Hotel. Check-in is surprisingly formal. The lobby is windowless and has a barrel-vault ceiling following the contour of the building. The clerk at the desk is a professorial type gentleman wearing a frumpy jacket with leather elbow patches and a black necktie.

He greets us, "Welcome to Resolute Bay. Do you gentlemen have reservations?" You'd think we had just stepped out of a Rolls-Royce.

"No, we just flew in. I know you've got a room for two, don't you?" Epps is still in his take-charge mode.

As we sign in, the clerk offers a suggestion, "There is a very nice dinner served next door at the Officer's Club. And as a guest here, you are entitled to full privileges there. There is one important thing, though. All guests must dress appropriately for dinner. "

I ask, "How appropriate is appropriate?" Even though my mind is thinking maybe I can make two neckties out of a red tee shirt I packed.

The clerk, still looking officious, responds, "Well, sir. It's not really difficult to adhere to the requirements. It simply means that one cannot wear blue jeans in the club."

"*Well, bully, bully.*" No. I don't say it. I only think it.

It's too early for teatime, so we go for one of our forced marches. This is a good way to both burn off unspent adrenalin and scope out the surrounding area. It's an energy-syphon thing that always works. But, as you know, you can't really burn off nervous energy. You can only mask it with exercise. So off we go, hoofing at a speed that just gets you breathing a little bit. Sure, this sounds like homespun corn, but Epps and I have done it for years. For us, it seems to work. And, no, we've never talked about it. Not even so much as this short paragraph. We just do it.

The surroundings of Resolute Bay are barren. The small cluster of leftover military buildings at the airport is little more than an ugly human remembrance on a moonscape of gravel. Piled and scattered here and there are dozens of rusted 55-gallon fuel drums. There are standpipes for a half a dozen in-the-earth fuel tanks. Among the rusted drums are pieces of wood pallets and old sheet metal scraps. One might say that the urban landscape is unkempt. But summertime in the Arctic must always be like this. Maybe it's best to see Resolute under the snow mantle of a nine-month winter. Nearly two of those months will be in total darkness. Maybe then it looks all nice and kempt.

There is still a low overcast, but the horizontal visibility opens up the vista to the water-expanse of the infamous Northwest Passage: the northern shipping link between Europe and the Far East.

At 600 miles north of the Arctic Circle, we're at the last outpost.

After an hour of hoofing it, we head back to the hotel to see if we can break out our khaki pants to wear to the Officers Club. It was just blind luck that we both brought a pair.

When we introduce ourselves to the tuxedoed doorman at the Club, he formally, but graciously, welcomes us into his establishment. This is bizarre. Even the waiters wear tails. Like us, the other patrons are dressed in flannel shirts, khakis and work boots. No ties or jackets. The interior décor is fitted out rather handsomely with tablecloths, thick carpet and heavy red draperies that create a kind of air-lock at the door. Tastefully framed prints are hung with an eye to artful decoration. Everything is pretty classy in here except the clientele. We don't know if it is code, chance or demographics, but there are no women around. There are six guys sitting at the bar and perhaps a dozen in the dining room that might hold 40.

The maître d leads us to a four-seat table with a linen tablecloth, a small plastic flower array, an ashtray and salt and pepper shakers. The waiter, who looks like a symphony conductor, comes over to take our order.

Epps orders first. "I'd like a white." Obviously he thinks he's still at The Downwind.

The waiter gives him a second look.

I pipe in, "That's code for wine, if one doesn't care what kind it is. So just make it a house chardonnay. I'd like a Labatt Blue, please." We clink glass to bottle, and Epps says, "One more time." He's not asking for another drink. OMT is an abridgement for *"Here's to Providence for looking over our shoulder one more time."*

I answer with a similar ceremonial response, "One more time."

We're definitely on a roll, but the flight tomorrow, weather permitting, is a long haul out to the end of the world and back. Anything can happen.

Before we order dinner, I catch the Conductor's eye and, with a hand gesture to the table, say, "One more time." This time it has nothing to do with Providence.

We consume the perfectly prepared steak dinner like we were still wearing blue jeans. By now we're relaxing a bit, and Epps is talking to some guys at an adjacent table. But when the pilot and crew of the Twotter stroll in, all eyes shift to them. They are in blue uniforms with stripes and wings, and their officer's caps are under their arms. The guys we're talking to at the next table know them and invite them over to sit with us. We all have a traditional snicker at the "hole in the clouds at the end of the runway" story.

The two pilots are our kind of guys. After their second pass, the one we heard while we were waiting for the fog to lift, they went back to their holding pattern and did laps for nearly an hour before taking another shot.

You gotta wonder if these guys might know the Oracles of Churchill.

Then they landed just like they were supposed to. I ask them about their low pass after we landed. They said they couldn't break the 200-foot minimum. Their smile tells the real story, and their attitude toward us expresses a manner of respect for how we handled our situation.

Of course, eventually, we get around to telling them about our plans to Roll the Pole. They look at one another like they know something we don't. Or maybe they have already had a conversation about us Yanks bumbling about in their territory. The Captain, who looks to be no more than about 25 years old, asks, "Now, how are you going to find the North Magnetic Pole? It's always moving, you know."

"Easy," I answer. "It's located on the aviation charts three miles off the north tip of Allard Island. The National Geographic map shows it twenty miles further northwest of the island. So we're going to split the difference and roll that point."

"Hate to disappoint you fellows," he answers, "but the pole isn't at either of those places. Right now, it's about 35 miles northeast of Allard Island. And that's a true bearing, not magnetic"

He and I do a quick sketch of the three Pole locations on a napkin. It's an elongated triangle. Before we leave, I stick the carefully folded sketch in my pocket for safekeeping.

The conversation gets back to flying stories, and these guys have got some great ones. Among other things, they've landed on gravel with skis and on snow on wheels. Epps and I listen. He and I have already blown more aviation smoke than we need to. Time for us to just coast.

At the next table beyond the Twotter pilots, there is an Asian guy sitting with a couple of locals. We pick up on their conversation. Now that all the eating is done, there are some great vibes going on in this room. It seems that this guy two tables over is Japanese, and he is solo-sailing a small boat through the Northwest Passage. We move closer to get the straight poop. His name is Yamasaki, and he doesn't speak English. Fortunately Epps can talk to him in Japanese; this is not difficult after two glasses of white. Epps opens, "Ah so. You no speekee Inglee? I no speekee Japanesy. You gotee boatee?" As bad as this sounds on many levels, Epps delivers it in such a friendly manner that, with short head bows, it is smilingly accepted.

Maybe Pat senses that Yamasaki, for the first time, perhaps, feels that somebody is sincerely interested in communicating with him at a visceral level.

The young adventurer is as sincere and shy as a monk. His eyes are a picture of focused concentration. But Epps's laughter and friendly claps on the shoulder prevail. Pat then gets the mariner to draw a map showing where his boat is moored. Epps tells him we are going to the Northee Polee in the mornee, and we'll see him in the afternoonee. One can only wonder what this kindly, solo, world-circumnavigating sailor is thinking.

The dialogue is a wonderful study in quasi-lingual communication. Pat draws a quick sketch of an airplane, points to a stick figure in the cockpit, then points to himself. Yamasaki smiles and draws a much better picture of a sloop with jib and mainsail set with an accurate profile of a man at the helm and points to himself. He says something in Japanese that, I'm sure, only Epps can translate. Then out come the maps. Yamasaki crossed into the Atlantic via the Panama Canal, sailed north and stopped at Resolute last fall. He then flew home to work through the winter and is now completing his journey. Pat's sketches of us going to the Magnetic North Pole may have lost a little clarity — but maybe not.

After a great evening at the Club, it's still daylight outside, as it will be for several more weeks. We crash in our beds at the Hilton, full and happy. What a splendid day.

The weather in the morning is excellent: scattered clouds are forecast for the next twelve hours. This is surely welcome news. We fire up the Bonanza and head 350 miles north to Allard Island. If all goes well, this should be a four-hour round trip. We don't even talk about taking the gyros and navigation radios out of the plane. We're going to follow our own logic on this one.

Finally, this is it. The last leg to the Pole.

The sun is behind us, so every 20 minutes we swing 45 degrees to the right to take a sun shot. The drill is quick and simple: first run the math and then change your heading just enough to get a shadow on the protractor. Then get back on course. We get it down to a 20-second gig.

At high noon, the sun will be due south. At midnight, it will be due north. At 6 a.m. and 6 p.m. the sun will be respectively due east or due west. These are rough estimates because time zones are wide and irregular. But for what we're doing, it works just fine. Basically we're flying visually, matching up islands on the surface with geographic charts. The fact that we have lots of identifiable islands here at the top edge of Canada, and the clear weather makes the visual navigation easy.

But I get to thinking, "Klondike, you know, it's been over two years since I rolled this airplane. Maybe I ought to get in a practice roll."

Pat's looking out the window at the ice flows between the islands and doesn't look up right away to answer my question about a practice roll.

"Then, practice it at the Pole. If you screw up, might as well do it there."

I'm also realizing that we have not secured a single piece of equipment in the back of the plane. We've got the shotgun, raft, tent, the cooler and that damned spare tire and wheel just lying around back there. If the roll does not go well, all these items can fly around the plane like a loose headache ball.

Even though everything right now is going along well, there is still tension in the cockpit. It's not between Pat and me. It's between us and the unknown.

The weather continues to hold fair. Man, what a treat! Two hours after leaving Resolute we are approaching the centroid of the three reported Magnetic North Poles. The magnetic compass stopped rotating 50 miles ago. No matter what direction we fly, it stays locked on 320 degrees. All the magnetic flux is now coming down vertically to the surface of the Earth. The compass needle is completely inert. It has no horizontal component.

Because we have profiles of two islands on our chart matching the two outside the window, we're able to triangulate the third reported Pole position, the one given to us last night by the Twotter pilots.

Finally, we're there.

It's August 12th, 1980, and 12:37 p.m. local time. The weather is scattered to broken with clouds at about 3,500 feet. We're at 7,500 feet, and the temperature at this altitude is right at 19° F.

With the exception of the one in this airplane, every operating magnetic compass in the whole world is now pointing right at us. And with the exception of the Arctic Ocean extending to the north, the world outside doesn't look one bit different than it did 100 miles ago. I force my mind's eye to see this one lonely, little lost gnat of an airplane about to do some aerobatics at this lonely end of the planet.

From your lofty vantage point, you can easily watch all of these goings-on. But you just gotta be wondering: is this really the stuff that dreams are made of? The quick answer: obviously, for us is, it is.

"Because it's there," was enough for Sir Edmund Hillary when he asked about why he had climbed Mount Everest. So why Roll the Pole, you ask? One answer is, "Because it's never been done before. And nobody knows, for sure, what the mag-compass will do inverted at that location."

But, there is another question lurking here in the cockpit, the question of who will roll the Pole first. There is only one control wheel in this airplane. This issue has never been broached between Pat and me. Not a word. And now, on the third attempt to get here, at 7,500 feet, we've arrived.

Who goes first must finally be addressed. We're both thinking about it. We both know it's time for a decision.

The only words spoken between us at this point are, "You take it."

"Got it."

To pick up airspeed, the nose of the plane is pushed over to put the nose just a little below the horizon. The power stays at cruise setting. The airspeed needle inches up to redline. The altimeter starts to wind down. A firm pull on the control wheel and the nose rotates up a little above the horizon. At just the right nose-high angle, the control wheel is rotated to the left, all the way to its stop. The right wing arcs up past the vertical and over we go. We come out at exactly 7,500 feet still on the same heading. A perfect roll. We bank sharply to make a smooth 180-degree turn and line up on the Pole once more but in the opposite direction.

"Let's do it again!"

The single control wheel is mounted to a central shaft that goes into the instrument panel. We pull a little unlocking release and rotate the wheel over to the other pilot. The nose goes down, airspeed increases, nose up and over we go. Perfect again. Now we have each rolled the Pole, both textbook maneuvers. Both of us get A's.

But then, unscripted, the second pilot, who still has the control wheel, whips another 180- degree turn, dips the nose again, pulls the nose up a little and rolls the pole a third time. This is way too much fun.

When we were at the top (inverted) of Epps's roll, I took a 35mm photo of the magnetic compass just to record what it did in that positive G position. It was still locked at 320 degrees no matter what direction (or configuration) we flew. So now you know!

Our conjecture is that the compass has found the composite magnetic field of the airplane. Or maybe it was just stuck on its last heading before we entered the magnetic Cone of Uncertainty.

This is the directionally dead space directly over the Magnetic Pole region.

In the end, one of us rolled the Pole first and the other unrolled it first and then rolled it the most. We shake hands and take the Sacred Arctic Oath of Silence. What I have just described here is all anyone will ever know about who did what first at the Magnetic North Pole on that beautiful August morning, 1980.

But something larger than the simple aerobatics of this flight just took place. Our feeling of accomplishment is probably no bigger than anyone reading this account has imagined. I think we can all agree that the accomplishment of Rolling the Pole is not earthshaking. It's simply executing a sophisticated aircraft maneuver in as remote a place in the world as we could find.

So Big Deal, a sceptic might say.

But it *is* a big deal. Something quite remarkable has transpired. Something Epps and I are only vaguely aware of at this moment. It is still in its embryonic form but, because of this adventure, our two destinies will be changed forever. This singular accomplishment exemplifies the dignity of man's efforts to expand his horizons beyond everyday life. With perseverance, any one of us can leverage that creative power to achieve, if not the impossible, at least the improbable.

In the olden days, this was called a *rite of passage*: the transition between one set of experiences to a more elevated set. At the very least, it is a self-certification of confidence: a new self-assurance that, with determination, we can play in this Arctic icebox with the best of them.

We may be too arrogant, and we may be very wrong, but that's how we feel.

Pat and I have changed from being those guys sitting under the wing of a plane, two years ago, trying to dream up something crazy. We are now two guys who have accomplished one of those crazy notions. It took three tries, hundreds of hours, and thousands of dollars. It took flying through weather as rotten as it gets (well, almost). It took stretching the limits of safety to the breaking point. And, most of all, it took perseverance.

Neither of us is yet aware of this transition. We are still occupied with getting our asses back to Resolute. We're now focused on the immediacy of visually navigating back to the only airport within fuel range. If the weather closes down, it could be an issue of consequence. Climbing down the mountain can be just as dangerous as the ascent. Now we can hear those little engine noises we blocked out earlier. Now we can see the cloud buildups to the south that we conveniently ignored. There is still the unsecured equipment in the back of the plane that we glossed over.

In the back of our minds, we both agree that the Arctic has an anomalous attraction that has captured both of our imaginations. Before, we were just Georgians, where the air is thick with the fragrance of flowers, pollen, microbes, freshly-cut grass, BBQ fumes and sweet pollution. All the good stuff needed to fuel a man's soul. Today, we've inhaled a different air.

There is something really quite captivating going on up here in the Arctic, where the only green is either American dollars or very thin lichen. For some unexplainable reason, we find Mother Nature's Arctic indifference and inhospitality to mankind as fascinating as it is menacing.

There is no question that today's compelling Polar success has given us mental license to expand our horizons beyond what they were yesterday.

We don't know it yet, but that expansion starts tomorrow.

But let's not get ahead of the story.

We bank the plane left toward the sun and start taking sun shots. I'm Left Seat this leg, so Pat's navigating. He's keeping a finger on the visual charts. We carefully pick our way back to Resolute.

The two-hour return flight turns out to be an easy one. In a little over an hour, we pick up Resolute's radio beacon. We've got it made now. We're back in the electronic world. But I still cannot unwind.

After we land and taxi up to the fueling station, the line attendant in his brown insulated jumpsuit comes out to flag us in. I jump off the wing behind Epps, rush over, shake his hand, and ask enthusiastically, "Hey, man. Do you know what we just did?"

"No. What?"

"Man, we just Rolled the Pole!!!"

He just looks at me and says, "Oh yeah? Well, how much gas you want?"

I am reminded, in one brief sentence, one more time, that what is important to one guy may not raise an eyebrow of the next.

I pay the tab for the Quonset Hut Hotel in cash from our money pouch, write down the expenditure on a small note pad and stick the receipt in a second compartment. When we get home, Epps and I will split whatever money is left over. We never tally up either the receipts or the accounting notes. Neither one of us knows whether I do a good job or not.

But Epps hasn't said *sayonara* to his Japanese friend. So we dump our bags in the plane and start hiking down a gravel road to the Inuit village a few miles away. We stick out our thumbs to the only vehicle driving by and catch a ride in a small, well-worn, once-red, Toyota pickup truck. The air is chilly but luckily there's only a light wind. When the truck stops to pick us up, I figure we'll be assigned to the truck bed in the back. But the driver waves us into the cramped cab. It does have a bench seat, though.

He's kind of scowlly and seems deeply involved in thought. We go along with the mood and don't mention the Pole thing. The heater feels good; we settle for that and don't talk. We thank him appropriately when we get out. He then waves goodbye and shows a huge, toothy smile like he had just played a trick on us. I have no idea what that was all about.

The village turns out to be a cluster of a half-dozen, two-story apartment buildings. Surprisingly, their architecture makes them look like they belong in American suburbia. They all have the same reddish-brown board-and-batten siding, small aluminum framed windows and pitched roofs with composition shingles. There is no effort to encourage landscaped vegetation.

As we walk between the buildings, we come across an Inuit-looking fellow sitting on a five-gallon bucket putting Teflon runners on a 10-foot long wooden dog sled. He's swarthy, weathered and comfortable-looking in his dark blue insulated jacket. He looks up at us from his work with a friendly smile. His leathered skin is stretched taut with long vertical creases coming down from his eyes. He says, "Hi, how you doin'." I'm only mildly saddened that Epps won't get a chance to add another language to his linguistic repertoire. The Inuit's perfectly normal, accent-free

English really is a little disappointing. We talk about his sled for a while. He takes a lot of pride in it and in his workmanship. He doesn't miss a stroke with his hand-plane while he's talking to us. When we tell him we're looking for the Japanese yachtsman who is sailing the Northwest Passage, he knows all about him. He points us down a narrow gravel road to a path that leads to a concrete ship dock. (No, that's not a dock for concrete ships. You figure it out).

The crisp, white 32-foot sailboat is conspicuous against the gray day. She's tied up outboard of a rusty gravel barge that's moored to the concrete dock.

For some reason the boat's main sail and jib are set. Maybe he's airing them out from winter stowage.

We clamor over the barge, and Epps stretches over the gunwale of the sailboat to knock on the cabin door. After a moment's bustling inside, the hatch to the cabin slides opens and there emerges the most perfectly composed, radiantly smiling Asian Princess you can imagine. Epps greets her in his peculiar Japanese vernacular, and she continues to display her sparkle. She smiles and flutters a little bit. Of course I cannot understand her reply to my buddy. Then, over her shoulder comes a smiling Yamasaki. He and Epps speak in their special lexicon and the only word that sounds anything like English is "solo." Yamasaki says, "Solo." Epps says, "Solo." They're both laughing and raise one finger. Not to be left out, I say, "solo," raise a forefinger and try to laugh too.

Epps and I have mused over this incident many times. Our conclusion is that "solo" in Japanese must mean that you take only *one* honey with you.

With one last, "Goodee luckee," Epps nimbly reverts back to his native tongue, "C'mon, lez go."

We start hoofing the three miles back to the airport on the gravel road. The daylight is good for another couple of weeks, so heading back south late in the day isn't a problem. We've finished our mission to the Pole, and I'm thinking a leisurely flight back to Atlanta will be most welcome. Maybe even boring. The first leg back to Baker Lake will only take a couple of hours. Then it gets easier and easier.

At the Met station at the Resolute Airport, we're told that the weather for the whole of the Northwest Territories is good for visual flying.

But apparently Epps has got another a bee in his bonnet. After leaving him for thirty minutes, while I go off to scare up junk food, I walk back into the middle of a phone call. It's not to home. It's with the Base Commander at Thule Air Force Base, *in Greenland*! I can only hear half the conversation. "Yeah, Colonel. It's just that I heard about Thule and I've never been there. Thought maybe we would stop by. What's the chances you setting up something for us to land there tomorrow."

There's a short pause, then he answers, "It's a Bonanza."

Another pause. "Well, if that's the way it is, maybe we'll just not visit." He hangs up not entirely un-abruptly.

I ask, "What's this Thule business?"

"Oh, nothin'. But since we're going to Greenland I thought we'd just start at the top and work our way down to the bottom tip."

"Greenland? I thought we were headed back to Atlanta. "

Pat answers, "Well, we are. But I'm going to Greenland first. And if you wanna come along, you're welcome."

He didn't exactly say, "This is my airplane," but it amounts to the same thing.

I have to ask, "So what did the Colonel say about landing in Thule? That might be kinda neat. They gonna let us do it?"

"He said sure we could land there. But if we do, they'll confiscate the airplane."

"Then I guess we know why he's stationed in Thule. Probably for attitude adjustment therapy."

And speaking about attitudes, now I have to figure out what's going on Pat's mind. This junket to Greenland that he's talking about isn't anywhere in the script. It has never been in Pat's DNA to share his thinking for the benefit of other people's curiosity. But this is a little off the scale.

In the meantime, the disappointment in not heading directly home gets lost in the prospect of exploring the west coast of Greenland. This might add a day to the trip, but it's really not all that far out of the way.

Pat, of course, then makes a case that this detour is my fault. Yeah, right.

From my 1977 journal, the story goes like this:

In June 1977, Pat, Zip, Mike Pickett, and I were ferrying a twin engine Piper aircraft to a customer of Pat's in England. All four of us being pilots, we rotated the Left Seat duties. The longest overwater flight was Pat's leg. I was in the seat directly behind him. We had just flown 750 miles from Goose Bay, Labrador, to the big airport at Narsaruaq, Greenland; it's about halfway between Nova Scotia and England. Unexpectedly, when we arrived over the airport, it was socked in. From our altitude above the clouds, we could see the pattern of mountaintops

*surrounding the runway protruding through the under-
cast. I matched the peaks with the approach plate chart
and felt confident that I could guide us right up the fjord
to the airport. I pleaded my case, but Pat wouldn't listen.
The other two pilots also had differing opinions as what to
do next. The fuel situation was becoming critical. Epps,
however, wouldn't just leave the area and fly another 450
miles to the next-closest airport at Kulusuk, Greenland.
Kulusuk is truly in the middle of nowhere on the east
coast of the island. He kept circling Narsaruaq, and it
was driving me berserk. An energetic discourse followed
about pissing or getting off the pot. His response was to do
another slow circle above the clouds looking down for any
entry opportunities to this airport. Finally, Pat capitulated
and headed northeast.*

*I resolved myself that we would not make it, and that
we would belly-in on the icecap.*

*Nonetheless, the flight across Greenland and then
cruising up the east coast was one of sparkling beauty.
The glaciers look like snapshots of flowing white lava
oozing down to the ocean. Nowhere on this flight was
mankind's footprint to be found. We see only the magnif-
icence of nature untouched. When we finally landed at
Kulusuk — two and one-half hours later — the gauges for
all four fuel tanks read E.*

That was three years ago. Since then I've ragged him about
not getting into Narsaruaq when I told him we could. Now Pat is
taking me hostage to watch him complete his mission — his way.

In his novel "Fate is the Hunter," pilot and writer Ernie Gann described the three almost identical, parallel fjords at Narsaruaq. At the ends of two of those fjords lie the scattered remains of broken airplanes that didn't find the one with a long beautiful runway at the end. Another story claimed that the old DC-3's came in through the soup so low that the ends of their 100 foot-long high frequency antennas would drag in the ocean. That's how they would know when to level off.

Back to now:

Well, obviously, Epps is a sucker for all this romantic stuff, and now he's out to prove what he's made of. Especially after how I ragged him so much about not even trying to land there with me guiding him in. Me, his 'ole buddy and fountain of wisdom.

Because of this friendly jibing, we now have to go all the way to Narsaruaq to help him redeem his honor. And I have to go along. Was it Brer Rabbit who said, "Don't throw me in that briar patch"?

Besides, as Epps points out, he *had* laid out the ground rules two years ago under the wing of Zip's plane at Oshkosh.

Although we don't know it yet, the real flying adventure still lies ahead.

CHAPTER 5

THE POLE HAS BEEN ROLLED

KALAALLIT NUNAAT

(Greenland motto: Inuit for "The Land of the People")
Resolute Bay, Canada, August, 1980

FOR ONE REASON or another, we're different guys than we were yesterday. It's not that we're more full of ourselves, or that we think we can do anything we couldn't do before. Or even that we are now experts on the Arctic or better pilots than we used to be. But the good feeling has something to do with the confidence that comes from setting an unlikely goal and achieving it. For two years we have been looking into the doubtful eyes of friends who thought we needed to have our heads examined. On the other hand, we are not nearly as elevated by this adventure as we are unburdened of the responsibility to complete it. Whatever it is, it feels good. From up there, where you're watching, you probably have a far better perspective on all this than we do.

Back in the Resolute Airport O Club (still no jeans), Pat and I lay out a course to fly due east along the top of Baffin Island and then curve around south along its easterly coastline. To have the shortest flight over water, we'll jump over to Greenland at the narrowest section of the Davis Strait. Even with an inflatable yellow life raft, ditching in icy Arctic waters offers only a marginal opportunity of survival.

Flight Service at Resolute Bay is a small office with a desk, a layout table and some radio transceivers. This time I ask the two guys on duty about taking instruments out of airplanes before flying over the Magnetic Pole. I know this is after the fact, but I want their opinion. They have no idea what I'm talking about. So much for another Arctic legend. The Flight Service guys don't have many folks to talk to, so they indulge us with an extra-thorough, almost chatty, weather briefing. The forecast indicates visual flight all the way to the town of Pond Inlet. This township lies on the north coast of Baffin Island, but it's still well above the Arctic Circle.

The aviation chart shows Pond Inlet to have a gravel runway with aviation fuel available. The distance from Pond Inlet to Resolute is 360 miles. With the boost from a little tailwind, it's an easy two-hour flight. The measure of sightseeing pleasure up here is calculated in how much tundra you can enjoy. On the other hand it's kind of crazy how pilots never get tired of looking at cloud formations. Some clouds look like animals. Some are mountains. Some are layers in a vanilla cake. Others look as if they are internally lit, and some even look like a Disney dragon breathing fire. Then, of course there are the angel clouds. These have an electric gilded profile from the sun glowing from behind them. They're everybody's favorite.

When you're eight or ten thousand feet up, mother Earth tends to break down into land, mountain or water masses. Except when you're inside one, clouds can be anything you want them to be. Last year's nearly four hours spent inside the dark belly of one big, black cloud mass with neither navigation nor communications will forever be imprinted in my memory as way too much of a good thing. I'm rambling here. Sorry. But I think you get the picture.

Coming up on Pond Inlet, we circle the town and spot their gravel strip a mile or so away. It's out in the middle of not-much-going-on. There are no hangars, work sheds or other evidence of human enterprise. The only intrusion on this Arctic wasteland is a 4,000-foot gravel scar on the tundra. Pat's driving this leg, and he rolls the wheels on the gravel without giving one the first inkling of touchdown. The gravel makes the tires just start rumbling. Nice.

Other than this raw runway and the gravel road leading north, even close up, there is no evidence of a human presence anywhere within sight. And, of course, there are no trees or shrubs nor babbling brooks, either.

This lack of human presence makes our arrival feel a little awkward. With no fuel storage tanks, fuel trucks, an operations shack, or even a tie-down area, the airfield feels woefully forgotten. It also raises a critical question, where do they store their fuel? The first thought that goes through my mind is, if the westerly wind abates, we should have enough fuel to get back to Resolute. If it doesn't, we have an issue to address.

We each pull out a hand-duffel. There are neither wheel chocks nor tie-down hooks in the parking area, so we set the hand brake and make a mental note to keep an eye on the wind. Pat locks up the plane, and we start hiking to town.

Along the sides of the rather rough gravel are small but beautiful blue-violets. They're so delicate that at first you don't notice them at all. But once you see the first one, you realize they're everywhere. Other than mowing the lawn, neither one of us knows much about botany. These little violets have got to be as tough as fireplugs to flourish here. A pleasant thought comes to mind, so I dig one up and fit it carefully in my jacket pocket. Later I'll put it in a plastic bag and take it home to Nancy. My other pockets have rocks in them. I collect rocks like other people might collect picture post cards. But common rocks, even polar rocks, don't have a great history for moving women's hearts. There is always a chance that an Arctic violet just might.

But there's no need to drag out the flower story. By the next morning, the plant looks like it's been dead for a week. The rocks, on the other hand, still look good.

The mile walk down the gravel road is just about the perfect distance to get our blood circulating. The air is crisp and clean, and our pace is brisk. The trek ends up in the middle of downtown Pond Inlet. Entering the village proper, we see that it is larger than Resolute by several factors. The street signs are in Inuit, and some have graffiti obscuring the script. The gravel roads are laid out on a strict engineer's grid. We're welcomed to town by a rustic but prosperous looking Hudson's Bay Company department store. It's a Wild West-style wooden building with a big front porch cluttered with boxes, pelts, chairs and other household goods. In the next block, we approach a two-story structure bearing a big sign that says "Hotel." Things are already looking up.

The entrance door of the hotel opens into a windowless vestibule with dozens of boots standing dress-right-dress along the walls. Upon stepping into the lobby, a comely Inuit woman, maybe a cleaning lady, gently suggests that we go back out to the vestibule and put our boots in line with all the others. Respectful of her admonitions, we de-shoe and make our second entrance. Every overstuffed chair and couch in the large lobby/living room is occupied. There are probably fifteen crusty old men, all wearing jeans, flannel shirts and heavy woolen socks. All thirty eyes look up at us. The atmosphere makes me think of a retirement home or a psycho ward. Or a funeral parlor. Everyone is reading. No one is talking or playing cards. There's no TV, radio or Muzak playing in the background.

It's 8:30 p.m. and, as you remember, the sun will not set tonight.

I go over to the gentleman behind the desk at the sign-in counter. "Good evening. We just flew in from Resolute, and we're looking for a room with twin beds." Just to be clever, I think, *with a view,* but I don't say it. There are people watching.

He looks like another displaced Torontoan doing *his* time in Purgatory. In a matter-of-fact tone, he states, "We have no rooms available, sir. The Canadian Government is conducting a survey of Pond Inlet, and the hotel is fully booked until October."

I sense that he's proud that they're full. I respond, "That's great. Business is good. Can you give us directions to another hotel?"

"This is the only hotel in town, sir."

He leaves it at that. The lobby crew is now all ears, and no one is reading. They have become fully engaged in our walk-in, road show. No one even tries to look away. In unison, their two-and-a-half dozen eyes shift back to me. My turn to talk.

141

"Okay, how about a guest house, or a boarding house?"

"Sorry, sir. This is the only place to stay in Pond Inlet, and we're full."

I swear he's proud of this fact.

I look to Epps. He shrugs. "So we sleep in the plane."

Just then, as if scripted, the curtain rises on Act Two. There is a break in the stalemate. A new figure walks out of the vestibule, sans boots, of course. He is a fully uniformed, perfect soldier-image of the Royal Canadian Mounted Police. Except for the stocking feet, we're looking at the only uniform that competes with the military dignity of a United States Marine in parade dress.

The Mounty is all business. There is no facial movement as he sizes us up. He moves only his eyes. First at me, then at Epps, then back to me.

"Are you the two gentlemen who just landed?" There is a measured tone, spoken in almost a stage voice. (Could it be for the audience?)

"Yep, about an hour ago," Pat answers with a smile. I would have added "Sir." Even though he had been a Captain in the Air Force, Epps doesn't bother much with military protocol. I, on the other hand, was an Army Airborne Infantry grunt. Having been required to salute everyone above me (which was just about everyone), I am still genetically disposed to pay more attention to military etiquette.

The Mountie then looks squarely at Pat, "So what seems to be the problem?"

"Ah, there really isn't any problem. We thought we might stay here, but we're hearing they're full up."

"Yes, they're full here so where do you fellows intend to stay?"

"Oh, well maybe we'll just camp out, sir" I offer.

"You know camping is not allowed around here without a permit. So what are you planning to do?"

"Maybe we need to ask for some help." Epps actually says these words! I can't believe it.

Some years after this incident, in a moment of relaxation, Pat told me that when he entered Georgia Tech, new students were given a battery of Vocational Aptitude Tests. He scored highest in Social Work. And this is at the Ramblin' Wreck school! Pat went ahead and gutted it out in mechanical engineering, but the people-to-people thing is still in his DNA.

And it's about to crank up here in the Pond Inlet Hotel lobby.

The Mountie then introduces himself as Corporal Oates. He and another Mountie are in charge of Baffin Island. Their territory runs from here all the way down to Frobisher Bay, 600 miles south. Talk about a beat!

"Well, you know, as it happens we have two cells in our jail here. Neither is occupied, and maybe I can arrange for the use of one of them for you fellows."

Jail never sounded so good. I resist the temptation to suggest that we commit a small crime to pay for the accommodation. The audience for my particular form of humor is really kind of limited, so (brilliantly) I keep my mouth shut a second time.

Even though Corporal Oates is strictly a no-BS guy, he seems sincerely interested in our welfare.

He asks, "How about aviation fuel? You fellows okay?"

"Well, we need to make it to Sondrestrom, Greenland tomorrow. That's about 900 miles. We really do need to get topped off." Pat's going for the brass ring.

"I assume you know that there is no fuel for sale in Pond Inlet. The only aviation fuel on the island belongs to the Queen."

As I said earlier, I had checked the charts before we left Resolute, and they said otherwise. Again, I keep my mouth shut. No avgas can be a much bigger problem than beds and clean sheets.

I'm trying hard to remember the next closest airport that might have fuel. If we must, we can always wait for favorable winds and fly back to Resolute Bay. Maybe we can add auto gas to what we have in the tanks and fly at fifty percent power.

Pat asks Oats, "You got any ideas?" I told you that he's a people-guy.

Oats hesitates as he thinks. Then he asks, almost smiling, "You fellows like the Boy Scouts?"

Epps has a nose for these things. "Oh, man, I was a Boy Scout. I love the Boy Scouts. You ought to see all my merit badges. I used to go to camp up there in the North Georgia Mountains every summer…"

Sensing that this story can go on and on, Oats comes right back on cue, "That's interesting. We're in the middle of a Boy Scout fundraising drive here. Also, I might know where there could be a couple of barrels of avgas. But, of course, I can't sell them to you."

The connection between the Boy Scouts and avgas is not very obscure.

"Super. How about we contribute something nice to the Boy Scouts. Whatcha think?" The money belt is right under my long john shirt, a flannel shirt, sweater and my jacket. We started this trip with six thousand dollars in $100 and $20 dollar bills. Credit cards are not yet universally accepted this far north.

"Done," I answer. "Where's the hat?"

The "hat" turns out to be a large ceramic bowl on a sideboard in the lobby. I have no idea how to estimate an appropriate contribution, and all eyes are on me. Somehow it doesn't feel quite right for Pat and me to huddle in front of everybody. Nor does it seem right for me to take out a pencil and calculate fuel cost and tonight's accommodation. It's clearly wrong to ask for a number and negotiations are out of the question. I simply have to come up with something convincing. I walk over to the bowl, turn my back on everyone, half disrobe, dig into the pouch and pull out three $100 bills and another $300 in $20 dollar notes. Folding the bills once, I put the cash in the bowl. Corporal Oats does not count it. In fact he doesn't even look at it. It is deemed satisfactory simply on the basis of man-to-man trust. Does that not say something about character up here? Nor did Pat ever comment on it, then or later. I still don't know if he thought it was either chintzy or too generous. It is certainly open to criticism. If I were to guess, I would say that he simply elected not to make any evaluations. The job got done without second-guessing, and now it's time to move on. That's a big part of Pat's MO.

The spectators in the lobby must hate for the episode to end. I bet they wonder how much went in the kitty. I still have the picture of all those eyes going back and forth in unison like spectators watching a tennis match.

It's a perfect drama. It has a plot: two lonely travelers are without lodging or fuel. It has action: a splendidly dressed Royal Canadian Mountie arrives to preserve order and then generously provides fuel and lodging. And it has a happy ending: the Pond Inlet Boy Scouts' fund-raising campaign prospers.

Pat and I pick up our bags and follow Corporal Oats up the gravel street to his immaculate jail. The municipal building is just like all the other structures in town: thick walls, few windows and a refrigerator door for entry. We leave our shoes at the door.

We're learning. The walls inside are painted semi-gloss white. The two steel-bar jail cages are open and face a time-worn desk just like in an old western movie. There are no wanted posters on the wall. The room is spotless with only the faintest hint of Lysol cleaner. The lettuce-green linoleum floor is kept brightly polished by the footsteps of stockinged feet.

Our luck holds, and we even get separate cells. Pat takes the cage in the corner, and I take the one next to the wall. We leave our overnight bags on our bunks, and Corporal Oates drives us back up to the plane in his pickup to fetch our sleeping bags. We three chat like old school chums on a vacation. Later, we unroll the bags on the thin mattresses which are on fixed iron cots. We would not swap this hospitality for a night in the Ritz. You wouldn't either. Guaranteed!

For dinner, Corporal Oates offers us ham sandwiches and an after-dinner lecture. The subject is a lesson in high Arctic Justice.

"The Inuit is not always a docile man. He'll flame up. He'll shoot another man if, in his mind, the circumstances have justified it. But our job is easy when dealing with a crime. We just ask the man if he did it or not. If he did it, he'll tell you. If he didn't do it, he'll tell you he didn't do it. But if somebody else did it, even though he might know who it is, he won't tell you anything. And you won't be able to badger him into telling you anything beyond his own actions."

"You mean if he shoots a guy, all you do is ask-around until you ask the right guy?" I ask.

"Yup. That's about it. Within the Inuit's community, they have disputes and strong disagreements, but very little larceny or petty crime. I'm sure you've heard stories about their lack of tolerance for alcohol. Well, it's true. They don't mix. Pond Inlet is dry, and we all respect that."

He goes on to describe his duties all up and down the hundreds of miles of the Baffin Island coast. The scale of his territory is staggering.

After a bit, I can't stand it a minute longer. "I gotta ask. Are you related to Captain Lawrence Oates of the Robert Falcon Scott expedition?"

He smiles. "Probably not, but I know the story."

The story goes that during Scott's return from the South Pole in 1912, Captain Oates was crippled by badly frostbitten feet. It slowed the progress of the last four survivors of the expedition. Supplies were running low. The wind was blowing fiercely, and the temperature hovered at -40° F. One night Oats said, "I am just going outside and may be some time." And then he left the tent without wearing his boots over his swollen and frozen feet. The others just nodded. They knew the man. Oats gave his life that night so that the three other men might have a chance to make it to the next food cache. But the weather never abated. The remaining survivors, including Scott, froze to death a few days later. Still in their tent, they were found the following summer. Scott left a note ending with the words, "these rough notes and our dead bodies must tell the tale."

Captain Oates' body was found only a few hundred yards away.

Since then, Oates' name has remained highly respected in explorer circles. I was hoping for a connection, but having to settle for meeting the "Oates of Pond Inlet" is just fine with Epps and me. Corporal Oates is not short in the least of any of the qualities we universally admire in men of adventure and duty.

As I put my head down upon the handkerchief-sized pillow, I cannot help but reflect. In this one day, we Rolled the Pole, flew a small airplane a thousand miles, walked three miles on tundra-lined roads in Resolute and sent off our friend, Yamasaki, to "solo" to Japan. I got kidnapped and now we're on our way to Greenland. We picked violets in the High Arctic. I put up with Epps the whole way, and now we are spending the night in jail! By any measure, it's been a day of notable proportions.

Early the next morning, Corporal Oates opens the jail and rousts us out of our bunks. It's 6 a.m. local and, of course, the sun is still above the northeast horizon. There is a hot shower adjacent to the office, so the day begins scrubbed and clean. Oates fries us bacon and eggs on a small counter cooktop. He then adds toast, coffee and more tales of the Arctic. And just think, we might have had the bad luck to have gotten a room with twin beds at the hotel.

Pat tells Oates that he wants to pick up a fox pelt like the ones hanging on racks behind some of the houses. Oates informs him that it is illegal to export pelts.

But he adds, "Pat, if you fellows want to go up to the Hudson's Bay Company, I'll go with you. I'll show you how to pick the best pelt. I'll also show you how to make a gun-bag. Fur gun-bags are legal to export. What you do with it when you get home is your business."

Epps nods conspiratorially, and the three of us hike up to the department store. After a brief tutelage on fur pelt selection, Pat buys a very nice gun-bag for the 20-gauge. That gun-bag now hangs — spread out trophy-fashion — on his paneled den wall in Atlanta.

The balance of the morning is spent exploring the Arctic charm of Pond Inlet. It is a remarkably civilized outpost with both pre-manufactured buildings and conventional architecture. The town looks down on a several miles-wide, inky-black inlet scattered with ice flows and many small, crystal-white icebergs. One uniquely large iceberg marches with the tides slowly east in the morning and west in the evening. It's a 30-foot tall, slow-motion sentry that reminds me of the guard at the Tomb of the Unknowns.

"We gotta go." Epps has either had his fill of Pond Inlet or the call of Greenland is beckoning. Actually, today's flight is going to be long and possibly treacherous. There will be no civilization, communications or electronic navigation for the next four hours. Navigation will be a combination of sun shots, our magnetic compass and whatever visual references we can find. This is my leg to fly, and it will have its measure of risk. But I, too, am ready to get on with it.

Before heading back to the airstrip, Corporal Oates drives us over to an outbuilding where we load a 55-gallon drum of aviation gasoline into his truck. The drum has been sitting there for who knows how long. Just to be sure it's okay, we filter the fuel through some cloth into a bucket then hand-pump it into the wing tanks of seven six Romeo. A quick goodbye to our friendly jail keeper, and we're on our way.

A month from now I will write a note to Prime Minister Pierre Trudeau thanking him for the Royal Canadian Mountie's hospitality. He writes back a short, personal note stating that Corporal Oates acted in a fashion that he expects of all of his Mounties. It was a nice comment, but I expected a little greater appreciation for our friend. We thought Oates was doing a hell of a lot more than just his job; not just with us, but with the community he served.

But, still, a note from the Prime Minister is not bad. It *is* personally signed.

The morning temperature is a few degrees above freezing, and there is a solid overcast at 1,500 feet. Visible moisture (clouds) and freezing temperatures are the perfect formula for putting ice on an airplane. Normally the air temperature drops about five degrees Fahrenheit per thousand feet of altitude gain. That means if we take off at 34° F. normally it will be 29° F. at a thousand feet. Keep in mind, however, that real weather doesn't always play by strict rules.

Icing on an airframe adds a little weight to the plane, but that isn't the main reason it brings them down. The problem is that ice changes the contours of both the wing and the propeller blades. Lift and thrust are both compromised; add a little weight and you've got a real problem.

In situations like this, Pat and I think alike. That is, if you're going to test a situation, have a Plan B ready at your fingertips. As I said, this is my leg, but just so there will be no misunderstanding about what the Plan B is, I lay it out.

"Here's the deal. We're going to fly just under the overcast at full power to build up airspeed. When we're flying as fast as I can get her going, I'm pulling back, and we're buying altitude about as fast as we can. We should either pop out above the clouds or get to where the temperature is too cold for moisture to form. No moisture, no ice."

"Humph, anything you want to do is fine with me." Epps says that, but I know damn well he's processing information like crazy; stuff like how much ice buildup are we going to get? How quickly will it happen, and will it be clear or frosty? Clear ice is the most lethal.

I go on, "I'm watching the altitude and airspeed, and you're watching the wings. If it comes on fast, call it and I'm pushing the nose over and getting back down to clear air below 1,500 feet." About the only good news concerning icing in a small airplane is that the problem doesn't usually last very long. That's also the bad news.

We level off at a thousand feet and start building up airspeed. I ease her up to the bottom of the overcast.

The throttle is all the way in to the firewall. It takes a couple of minutes to get up to max speed. When the airspeed needle hits redline, I ease back on the controls; not abruptly, but firmly. The whole idea is to be smooth. The world immediately goes dark in the overcast. Seconds tick by as the airspeed starts its steady bleed-down. Thoughts go into automatic hold. There is no conversation. Pat and I are in our own different worlds. We're not one mind with four hands; we're parallel universes with one destination. Time stops as we watch the airspeed indicator. It slowly inches down as the altimeter continues to climb.

If we can get the outside air temp down to 25° F. or colder, we can stay in the clouds. Otherwise we need to be in clear air.

Our luck holds. We pop out at 6,500 feet, one mile higher than where we entered the clouds. The airspeed is down to 75 mph; that's about ten mph above the Bonanza's stall speed. The world is brilliant blue sky above and sparkling white clouds below. I push the nose back down to level to regain airspeed. We can see nothing of the Earth beneath us, but the rest of the universe is now our oyster. It's a perfect insertion into space.

The windshield and leading edges of the wing have only a light coating of rime ice. There is no structural buildup. We're golden. It's amazing how so many of the small triumphs go unnoticed in our lives. Almost as quickly as they end, they're forgotten. But that's why we have me down here to write it all down and you up there to watch.

Since Thule Air Force Base didn't invite us to enjoy their little piece of paradise, we begin the nearly 900-mile non-stop flight to Greenland by flying down the east coast of Baffin Island. That's about the distance from Atlanta to Boston.

After an hour, the cloud deck below breaks up, and we are perfectly placed to see one of the most spectacular sights on planet Earth: the black stone coastline of Baffin Island. The ragged, hundreds-of-feet-tall rock face at the shoreline provides a dramatic contrast to the deep blue, almost black water of the Davis Strait. It looks like giant chunks of anthracite coal topped with whipped cream and floating in an ocean of blue-black ink. It also looks uniformly inhospitable.

There are no beaches, lagoons or places for either humans or animals to approach from the sea. Sea birds might be an exception to this. But from our perspective, it's all hostile territory. For three hours we fly along this coast mesmerized by the raw assertiveness of nature. But no matter how terrifyingly majestic Baffin Island is, we finally have to turn east and cross the Strait. This is a 250-mile over-water flight. Exchanging the brutal land for the freezing open water is a toss-up. Survival in either environment is more than problematic.

Since there is nothing else to do for the next few hours except hold heading and altitude, I ask Pat to steer while I read the fine print on the aviation chart. Under Sondrestrom, there is a note that aircraft landing for the first time in Greenland without an International Flight Plan will be charged $200. I bring this up to the co-pilot because when he filed our Flight Plan, he made no notation of this being "International."

"Klondike, all you had to do was check a box. I mean, how hard is that?"

"Don't worry about it," he says. "I'll talk to 'em, and they'll waive the penalty." He can get away with that sort of stuff. Me? I just roll over. If they ask for it, I pay it. Bucking authority is just another one of those things that Pat can do gracefully when he wants to. I can't help myself. I end up turning discussions with authorities into confrontations — confrontations that I lose, more often than not.

Sonde comes up exactly where it's supposed to — 15 miles right of the nose. I chirp the wheels halfway down the very long runway, but it's still a lengthy taxi to the fueling station. The two of us walk up to the service desk in the terminal. An attractive Danish woman in a tailored blue uniform and blonde hair in a tight French bun smiles at Epps. Right then and there he's toast. And we both know it.

"So sir, you know there is a two hundred dollar fee for landing without an International Flight Plan?"

Epps looks at me without expression.

"How 'bout giving the lady two hundred dollars."

This story is always fun to retell in Pat's company. Although he's heard it a hundred times, he still doesn't laugh. He's always so cocksure of himself until a pretty face with a little authority brings him back to earth. Man, I love it! My spirits are lifted!

Without pausing a minute, we polish off a rich, but super-delicious Danish-style buffet lunch in the airport-hotel cafeteria. Paying greenbacks for the fuel, we take off and head south along the west coast. Our destination is Gothab, the Capital of Greenland. Epps is Left Seat. The coastline along this route is rugged by any standard. It almost competes with the harsh, black rock of Baffin Island. Here the gentler, snow-covered rock formations have been cut with deep fjords. Those fjords have glaciers flowing slowly west toward the sea, where they either melt or calve off into icebergs. The icebergs then drift south into the Atlantic and lie in wait for Titanic's to lumber by. Greenland is why the Atlantic has icebergs and the Pacific doesn't. Think of it as a giant ice cube machine that perpetually overflows.

An hour out of Sonde, Pat gets a wild hair. He's tired of looking at all this raw nature. Now he wants to play Mister Hot Dog Fighter pilot. Pushing the nose over to build up speed, he proceeds to fly down the fjords like he's schussing at Vail. We're roaring down a great blue-iced crevasse, wingtips barely 50 feet off of the ice-flow walls, but it is the narrowness of that gap which grabs my attention. The airspeed indicator is pushing 200 mph and we're getting into some locations so tight that Pat needs to tip the plane up at an angle to squeeze through. At this speed, I cannot judge the distance of the wing tip to the ice walls. Hell, I can't make myself look anywhere except straight ahead. This is pure craziness. I share my opinion vociferously with Mr. Hot Dog himself. Eventually he backs off a little bit. With 100-foot wingtip buffers, the flight becomes enjoyable. Well, almost.

Flying down vertical-faced corridors will not be replicated for non-aviators until computer simulators do it in animations of space machines chasing frenzied three eyed Anti-gravitrons through the broken planet of Orxezizus. Or something like that. The problem is, here in a frozen fjord, this airplane ain't no simulator, and those rocks aren't virtual.

In defense of our friend here, he really is an exceptional pilot. He holds an Aerobatic Rating with Low Altitude waivers to fly in air shows. He also holds an Airline Transport Pilot's License. Of course, Pat has all the other Commercial, Multi-engine, Instrument ratings too. After his stint in the Air Force, he worked for Boeing as a Flight test engineer on big-ass bombers. He knows his way around airplanes with the best of them.

Still, for weaving pilot-tales in The Downwind, threading the fjord-needle is about as good as it gets this side of a lunar landing.

"Klondike, how 'bout we get a little altitude before we call Gothab. We need a better view of this coast line and some radio contact. Whatcha think?"

Finally, he seems to have satisfied his adrenalin dependency. We ease back up to 7,500 feet, and he calls the airport. "Gothab tower, November eight one seven six Romeo, forty miles north, inbound for landing."

They reply, "Roger seven six Romeo, the airport is closing in ten minutes."

We're still 20 minutes out. Inasmuch as I filed this Flight Plan, I tell Epps, "I'll take the mic."

"Gothab tower, N8176R, we filed a Flight Plan at Sonde direct Gothab with our ETA 1710 local. That Flight Plan was approved. This tells me that the airport will be open for us."

They answer, "Gothab tower, we close at 1700 local. If you wish to land, there is a $200 fee for staying open after hours."

I can't believe this. This sounds like an Epps setup to get even with me after goldilocks zapped us in Sonde for not checking the International Flight Plan box. But I'm not going to cave in.

"76 Romeo, we roger that. Go ahead and close. We'll land without a tower."

"Gothab tower, negative, the airport will be closed and the gates locked."

"76 Romeo, That'll be fine. We can crawl under the gate and settle up with you in the morning."

Long pause.

"Gothab tower, regulations require that we have a fire truck on standby before you land. Say your intentions."

I'm still on the mic. "Seven six Romeo. We waive the fire truck service. Ya'll go on home, and we'll be okay. We can land without a tower or a fire truck. We'll check in with you in the morning."

Longer pause. Different voice this time, "This is Gothab tower. If November 8176 Romeo intends to land at this airport, the fee is two hundred US dollars, payable upon landing. State your intentions." This sounds like the boss man.

I look at Epps, and he's just enjoying the hell out of where this has gone. This ticks me off even more. Damn it, we filed a Flight Plan and did everything according to the book. The Flight Plan had our arrival noted at ten minutes after five, local. The system should be satisfied. We should not be penalized!

"To hell with them," I say to Epps. "We've got plenty of fuel. Let's just go on to Narsaruaq."

"No, we gotta see the Capital. You work it out." He's still smiling. This is clearly payback time.

I get back on the radio. "Gothab Tower, November 8176 Romeo, if you will hold the airport open for 10 more minutes, we would be pleased to land…and pay the fee, over." Man, I hate this.

"Roger, 76 Romeo. Call the airport in sight."

"We've got you in sight now. We're five miles northwest."

"Roger, 76 Romeo. Cleared to land."

Pat is tickled like he did something wonderful. I'm steaming. I've also decided I'm not going to get over this humiliation until my second beer.

Macht nichts to me whatever brand they might serve here. But wait a minute. Greenland used to be Danish territory. I bet they will have Tuborg and Carlsberg.

The Danish-looking guy (i.e. blonde, black tie, blue eyes, white shirt and slim black trousers) behind the desk at the terminal accepts ten twenty-dollar greenbacks with the grace of a patient concierge. He displays no sign of victory. Politely, he recites a few airport regulations, and then we're on our way. He's being mister nice guy. I need to put this bologna behind me before I make things complicated. Pat's bouncy attitude helps not one bit.

The ten-minute Mercedes taxi ride into town is a pleasant break. The streets are paved and have curbs, streetlights and sidewalks. There are a number of roundabouts and abundant car traffic. Scattered here and there are struggling shrubbery or stunted trees. Every once in a while we even hear a car horn honking. Boy, does that bring you back quickly. There is almost a hint of European hustle in the air. The population of Gothab is about 10,000 folks; that's one-fifth of the total population of Greenland.

In 2010, Greenland has twice the population it had during the Medieval Warming Period a thousand years ago. That's when

Eric the Red raised cattle here and exported trees to Europe. Five hundred years later, the Little Ice Age took care of that enterprise, and the Norse population vanished or retreated back to Europe.

Much of the town is composed of three-to-five story, Soviet-style, institutional apartment blocks. Some old churches and marketplaces are scattered about. We check into a respectable, second class, well-worn Danish style hotel. They have a three-table restaurant and a five-stool bar. Without sprucing up we head out for a fast-paced evening tour. We're below the Arctic Circle now, so the sun will set tonight. You do remember that the "Circle" marks the boundary for the most southerly 24-hour summer day and the most southerly 24-hour winter night, don't you?

On the harbor shore is an open-air meat market spread out along a sidewalk. We stop to watch an interesting transaction, and it suggests a rich cultural divide that lies just beneath the surface. It's August 18th, and the air temperature is about that of a refrigerator — just above freezing. Hanging from a head-high wood frame are whole, raw, hindquarters of some animal about the size of a goat. They're lean, skinned and Ferrari red. A dozen carcasses are lined up for the choosing. We watch an Inuit guy negotiate for one. He makes a deal, and it is quickly wrapped in newspaper. In an easy heft, he raises it on his shoulder like an M-1 rifle and marches home to a family feast. The simplicity and honesty of the purchase is disarming. It is a direct point-of-sale transaction, neither elegant nor ugly. The lack of hygiene is definitely non-Western. It's the fundamental intersection of supply meets demand. Not many generations ago, that fellow's ancestors speared a musk ox, quartered it, and buried it along with netted birds still in their feathers and fish still in their scales. Everything was wrapped in walrus skins and stored in a snowbank.

Periodically, throughout the long, dark winter, he'd revisit his cache to feed his family. I wonder if this thought could be going through this man's mind as well. Not likely. Probably there's a soccer game playing on the TV in his cozy-warm but stuffy government-provided apartment.

The reality is that except for this meat, most of the rest of his family's current diet probably comes from Denmark. And it is undoubtedly pretty good. Like lunch today in Sonde, canned Danish food is tasty, rich and filling.

Once back at the hotel, Pat and I settle for well-prepared steaks that taste almost like Texas beef. It's still daylight, and town folk are still walking around in the streets when we hit the sack.

This morning we taxi to the airport early. I had paid our $200 penalty yesterday, and today I pay for the avgas and file a Flight Plan for Narsarsuaq, 380 miles to the south. Pat flies Left Seat again so he can make his obligatory approach into Ernie Gann's favorite airport; it's still that vindication thing. But this time we don't do any more of that hot dogging stuff. We'll fly just like our wives would want us to. Today we will *remember our responsibilities.*

The topography keeps changing as we fly south. There are now tidewater plains, islands and occasionally even open vegetation. The coast below is becoming the most forgiving we've seen in days. The shoreline is porous with infiltrations of inlets and hollows. The Davis Strait, hundreds of miles wide, lies off our right wing.

The weather all the way down to the southern tip of Greenland stays flawless — plenty of brilliant sunshine and unrestricted visibility. As we approach the southern climes surrounding Narsarsuaq, we can clearly see its three famous fjords. The terrain takes on a hospitable tone of green plant life and open pastures. Being held back by the mountains to the east, the frozen surface of the great white ice pack is clearly visible.

And then, up ahead, in a tightly packed cluster around an outlying island, I see a sailboat regatta! The white sails are following a course in a gentle curve and then spread out as they race for open water.

"Klondike, catch that sailboat race over there!"

"Got it."

He dips a wing and then the nose. I know what he's thinking. He wants to buzz the race! Astonishingly, it's more than a minute before we get close enough to both realize that the contestants in this event are a fleet of cottage-sized icebergs following an invisible current around an indiscernible course marker. The bergs are trapped in a giant ocean eddy.

I tell Epps, "Hell, man, I knew they were icebergs all the time. I just wanted to see how gullible you were."

He doesn't smile. Good. That means I got him.

Pat radios Narsaruaq and they clear us for a visual approach. As we follow the radio beacon up the fjord, we see a notation on the approach plate, "sunken ship." Sure enough, at exactly the right location, passing under the nose is the rusted hull of a ship half submerged in the fjord. We ease left a little and line up for the airport. Right in front of us is a beautiful 6,000-foot concrete runway.

Pat lets the plane settle onto the concrete surface in less than 1,000 feet, and we taxi right up to the Service Department door of a giant WWII-vintage hangar. Nobody is around, so he shuts the engine down. We climb out and jump off the wing. Everything having to do with the airport ground operation looks closed.

Then a security guard turns up and tells Pat he has to move the plane. The guard's manner is impatient.

Cranking up a hot engine in an airplane is not like restarting a car. It's a sequential routine having to do with cowl flaps, fuel cut-off, setting the mixture control and throttle adjustments. But Pat dutifully follows the guard's instructions and taxis to an out-of-the-way corner a hundred yards beyond the main hangar. This is not the most cheerful introduction to Narsarsuaq.

We walk a quarter of a mile to the Met office. The two-story facility has lots of glass, Danish modern furniture, a few large photographs on the wall and two personable meteorologists. The clean-cut young men running the office give friendly directions to the best local hostelry. Actually, there is no second choice, but another quarter-mile walk is welcome. The Inn reminds me of a mountain cabin style of motel that you might find in Montana. There's the requisite steep roof and knee-braced columns at the entrance, wooden exterior and almost no landscaping.

The exposed wood trusses and stone fireplace reinforce the feeling of an old lodge. After a dinner of beautifully prepared breaded veal cutlets, we hoof it back to the Met office. Other than the fact that this part of Greenland is greener than what we've seen farther north, the countryside around us reveals very little information. If there is a town of Narsarsuaq, it must be around the corner somewhere. The rolling rocky hills and protected harbors around here suggest a familiar setting in perhaps Maine or Nova Scotia.

Except for a reported 20-knot headwind, the weather over the North Atlantic looks good for tomorrow. The forecast for Goose Bay, Labrador is widely scattered clouds and good visibility. Built during WWII, Goose is now a bustling airport used as a refueling opportunity for transatlantic flights.

Mentally preparing for this long, over-water flight brings up some serious issues. For a safe conclusion, any airplane relies entirely on the dependable operation of a large number of complex mechanical parts and electronic circuitry. If everything works perfectly, the flights are quite safe. It is the failure of the smallest spring, a fatigued valve stem or a tired diode that brings on wet landings. This dependency on lots of small things working faithfully is doubly true with a single engine plane.

Before we leave the Met station, I figure it is a good time to call home. We've been gone five days. I did call a couple of days ago when we rolled the pole. Everything was good then.

"Mitch? Sorry for calling so early. Everything at home going okay?

"Oh, yes. We had a downpour yesterday but the roof didn't leak."

I think this remark is to make me happy. We live in a treehouse on a large, heavily wooded lot in Atlanta. I've never adequately solved the flashing where our four trees, Mathew, Mark, Luke and John, go through the roof. In fact, we still have raccoons come in the house through the sometimes-waterproof connection at the trees.

Nancy offers a patient and thorough rundown on each of the kids' activities. There is not a hint of her being left out of my life, or me out of hers.

Naturally, Nancy's quite interested in each phase of these travels. As a pilot, she appreciates the derring-do of aviation. Her personal flying style, however, is careful and by the book. In fact her entire lifestyle is pretty much that way. But her dedication to a sense of order does not preclude her appreciation of deviations from the norm. That's my job.

At the end of the call, I get my time-honored remonstration, "Remember your responsibilities," and, "we all miss you."

Pat called home last night, and I have no idea what the conversation was. That stuff is way too personal for us to talk about.

At the Met Station, first thing in the morning, Pat fills out the Flight Plan in his usual offhand manner. He only hits the highlights like destination and time of departure. The very nice guy running the desk there checks over Pat's half-assed job.

In a pleasant voice, "Mr. Epps, for type of aircraft, you wrote F33A. Please fill in the correct ICAO designation." ICAO stands for International Civil Aviation Organization. They set the standards for international flights.

"It's a Bonanza F33A. I wrote F33A. Come on, Super. Lez go."

Well, damn! Here we go again.

The Met man is not going to let this thing go either.

"I'm sorry, Mr. Epps. For this flight plan to be official, it must be filled out completely and properly. I need the ICAO number."

"Well, in the Type of Aircraft box, I put down F33A because that's what it is. If you want to call it something else, feel free. Come on, lez go."

He heads out the door, but I stay behind to oil the waters.

I offer, "The problem is we don't know the ICAO designation. If you have a Regulation book, I'll be glad to look it up."

… what a guy has to do sometimes.

163

It takes me five minutes to figure out the correct designation, fill out the Flight Plan properly and apologize for one of our attitudes. Then I double-time out to the plane. Pat has been talking to the same security guard/ lineman we met yesterday. Pat's body language indicates he's still got the red-ass.

"Klondike, you can relax now. I got the Flight Plan all worked out. You got the plane fueled?"

"The plane's okay. You're driving. Climb in. We're outta here."

There is something very wrong going on. I think it's bigger than the ICAO thing.

I ask. "Okay, what's the deal?"

"They're not selling us any gas unless I declare an emergency. Well, that's bullshit! We don't have an emergency. We just want to buy some damn gas. They're acting like assholes. Come on, lez go!" By nature, Pat is ordinarily very stingy with his personal epithets. It's like, for a high school graduation present, his mother gave him a hundred curses to last a life time, and now he's getting low. As far as I know, this little cluster of abuses is a new personal best for him.

"Well, guess what? It will be an emergency if we get halfway to Goose and run out of gas. I'm gonna go talk to the guy."

Pat leaves me standing and walks directly over to the plane. Over his shoulder, "I figured it out. We got a half-hour reserve. Besides the winds aren't as bad as they said."

Well, damn. When he starts juggling facts to match his argument, he is usually remarkably successful. But it can still be incredibly dangerous. To compound the problem, he is also in his lez-go mode. "Lez Go" can also be interpreted as, "Be-damn the torpedoes."

This is not good. But a frontal attack between the two of us is out of the question. "All right, let's get in the plane and do a thorough fuel calculation together."

He agrees. I'm in the left seat. Side by side we get out the charts and a clean sheet on my kneepad.

Using statute miles, the flight to Goose Bay is 782 miles. The headwind at 9,000 feet is forecast to average 20 knots, say 25 miles per hour. This will give us a ground speed of about 165 mph and will take 4.7 hours. With full fuel and the reserve tank full, the Bonanza has 7.0 hours' endurance.

Yesterday we flew 1.8 hours from Gothab here to Narsarsuaq. Adding that to the 4.7 for today's flight equals 6.5 hours. This will leave us with half an hour of fuel in reserve. Epps' comment on headwinds is pure smoke. But, there is also another consideration: the last 140 miles will be over Terra Firma. If things go against us, at least we'll land on tundra. Soft tundra, I hope. And, remember, we do have survival gear. Besides, it is his airplane.

"Okay, Klondike, I'm with you. We'll stay high and lean the engine down to a gnat's ass and see if we can squeeze out a little more reserve."

I crank up the engine and call ground control. Right now Epps doesn't need to be talking to anybody but me.

As we taxi out, I go through CIGAR TIP. This is an old-time pilot's acronym for a pre-takeoff checklist. **C**ontrols, **I**nstruments, **G**as, **A**ltimeter, **R**un-up, **T**rim Tabs, **I**nterior, **P**assengers buckled in and know how to get out the window.

Finally, imperfect as this departure is, we're on our way back to North America!

To save fuel, I make the climb-out as long and gradual as possible. We use takeoff power for only one minute then immediately go to long-range cruise settings. We start leaning the fuel mixture even before we're out of the fjord. We're going to lean this baby for all she's worth. The weather is beautiful. Emotions are secure. Even the ol' Grouch is simmering down.

In 45 minutes, the last image of Greenland's rugged mountains and magnificent ice cap fades below the horizon. In another 30 minutes, we lose electronic navigation and radio contact with the rest of the world. The over-water portion of this flight is 610 miles. It's really peaceful up here. The motor is leaned out but running soothingly. Epps reaches back to the reserve tank and twists a couple of valves so we can run that tank out first. This permits the fuel gauges to tell us what is left in the wing tanks.

High overhead we watch the frozen contrails of airliners following the Great Circle Route from Europe to New York or Chicago. Their shadows leave long dark lines on the ocean surface 9,000 feet below us. It feels like we're riding on rails straight to Goose. There are hundreds of icebergs slowly making their way south to their North Atlantic playground. From our altitude, we can see no white caps. Although it's not, it looks peaceful and calm down there.

Time drones on. Pat catnaps in the right seat. Our only concern now is conserving fuel. We have no means to check what the headwind is doing to us. We can only hope it's not more than 20 knots. Every 20 minutes we guess our longitude and take a sun shot.

Then, out of the blue, **Sput ... sput ... sput**. The engine stumbles. My right hand goes straight for the auxiliary fuel pump, but Pat's left hand is already there.

I call out, "Check the fuel valves on the reserve tank."

Epps says matter of factly, "They're good. Fuel pressure's good. Oil pressure and manifold pressure's good. Hold your heading and altitude."

If the fuel pressure is good but the engine is starving, that's very bad. There is an auxiliary fuel pump, but we don't have a backup fuel injection regulator. Or maybe it's a broken fuel line.

I say, "I got us straight and level. How about pulling out the life raft and start pumping. Don't get it too big to get out the door."

The engine stops sputtering and then runs evenly. My anxiety level doesn't go away quite that quickly.

Pat unbuckles his seat belt and pulls the raft from the back seat and into his lap. He's looking around, "Where's the pump?" he asks.

"Hell, I don't know. You brought the damn thing. Blow it up by mouth. We just need something to get us to an iceberg. If we're gonna go in, I'll put us as close to a berg as I can."

The motor continues to run smoothly. Whatever made it gag may make it gag again. I get my binoculars out to look for the friendliest looking berg. With the binoculars, I can now see the white caps. We're not halfway across the Davis Strait. It is a calculated risk to keep going rather than turning back. The opportunities for rescue probably improve closer to Canada. The engine miss sounded like the cause was fuel-oriented. It was a stumbling sound. Maybe it's electrical but definitely not structural. An engine can blunder along for a long time with an electrical miss like a fouled spark plug. I wonder if it is a clogged fuel injector nozzle.

"Klondike. We goin' on, or we turning back? I think we keep going."

Without hesitation, he points to the windshield and says, "We goin."

Epps is puffing into the raft like a steam powered compressor. Actually, he looks good when his face is a little blue.

Fifteen minutes feels like hours. There is so much running through our minds that we hardly talk. I've studied every dial and gauge ad nauseam. So has my puffing buddy. Now everything is running normal and steady.

I'm still picking icebergs; I want something we can glide to and be closer to Canada. I try to get a sense of the wind direction on the surface from the wave action, but we're still too high. Little gusts of anxiety still blow through my brain and start to cloud my perspective. This is serious stuff. Epps looks serious, too. But we've done everything we can do. The old aviator aphorism for this kind of situation is a three word phrase: Avigate, Navigate, Communicate. Avigate means no matter what the problem is, fly the airplane first. Navigate? We're on "the Rails." There is no more thinking required for that item. Communicate? Pat starts calling 121.5 megahertz, the universal aviation Emergency Frequency. Maybe we can pick up an airliner and report our situation. After three calls in the blind, there is no answer. We're definitely out here on our own.

I look down for contrail shadows. There are none. Then I look up for contrails. There are none of those either.

I cannot speak for Pat, but my anxieties keep flowing back. To myself, inwardly, I ask something inside my brain like: *clear my head and steady my hand.* Maybe it's some kind of prayer or Yoga mantra or something. I don't know. But, for me, it always works. I'm back where I'm supposed to be. The nervous elements of fear and confusion vanish. As far as I know, Pat doesn't have to talk to himself like that. But who knows?

To you up there, I hope we look like just two guys tooling across the North Atlantic and that everything's cool.

It's now been 20 minutes since the sputtering. Finally I gotta ask, "Okay, Klondike, whatcha think?"

"You just keep holdin' your altitude and keep your heading. Everything's going to be just lovely."

"That's not what I meant. What's wrong with the motor?"

"Hell, I don't know. It just sputtered. What do you think?"

"I don't know either, but maybe there was a bubble in one of the fuel cut-off valves. If that was it, we're in good shape."

Epps' response is typical, "Yeah, that was it. We're in good shape. I told you so. And I'm going to quit blowing this damn thing up." He carefully stuffs the half inflated raft onto the back seat.

The motor continues to run without a hiccup. The gas gauges are not moving because we're still on the reserve tank, the one that maybe used to have a bubble in the valve. I hate to think about it but we've got to run this auxiliary tank dry. And the only way you know it's dry is when the engine sputters. Oh boy, I'd be happy **not** to hear that again. But there is really no choice. After it sputters, we will switch to the left tank and run it dry in the same manner. We then switch to the right tank and hope it never sputters until we land at Goose. We took off on the right tank so it's not full, but it's got a good gauge. This way we won't get into the situation where we are looking for a last drop of fuel in other tanks. When the last tank sputters, there is only one more decision to make: Avigate to the best crash site within gliding distance.

The truth of the matter is you don't want to run the last tank dry. You remember that trick, don't you?. You try to keep just enough fuel to make last-minute adjustments — like hanging on the prop to slow down before touchdown.

Canada is still somewhere over the horizon. The view of the undisturbed vastness of our magnificent planet is humbling.

Tired of trying to look over the horizon for a coastline, I pick an easier target: Pat Epps. Stretched out, all catawampus, right next to me, he's into his nap. He's pensive, not worried looking. Certainly not fearful. Even asleep he looks deeply thoughtful, and thoughtful is something you can't share. Well, that's enough of looking at him. I'm going back to the studying the horizon.

Finally the engine does sputter. Epps stirs long enough to switch to the left wing tank, and the motor picks right back up like it's supposed to. No words are spoken. He goes back to sleep. Well. He goes back to what looks like sleep. It might just be social withdrawal. Either way works for me.

The next two and a half hours go by with virtually no conversation between us. What's to talk about?

We're still over the ocean somewhere. There is no way of determining our position. We steer by magnetic compass heading and sun-shot guesses. As I said, we don't know where we are east and west. Well, for that matter, we don't know where we are north and south either. The airliner shadows are the best we have to steer by. Fortunately, they have returned. The jumbos at 35,000 feet have redundant gyroscopic inertial guidance systems for navigation. They don't even need magnetic compasses.

From up there looking down at us, I bet you admire our creativity in following those contrail shadows, don't you. Hang on, and we'll share the rest of this little learning lesson with you.

Canada is still not in sight.

I make myself take a big pause. This is a long haul; we're tight on gas, and we've had an engine glitch. But, you know what? We're still flying, and we're still in control. I make myself think positively. We're going to plant this airplane on the runway numbers at the Goose Bay International Airport, or worst case, very close to it. We're definitely going to make it! No question about that.

Our course stays steady on the invisible chord between the contrails above and their shadows below.

Then. OOOOOH, look ahead!

All along the western horizon lies a low, dark cloud-bank. That may signal land! Probably does. Timewise, it's overdue. The engine keeps humming, but then sputters. Epps switches quickly to the right tank and the engine relights immediately. This exhausts the fuel in the left wing tank. Our last tank, the right one, is less than half full. It is the one we used to take off with and to climb to altitude before switching to the reserve tank. But the gauge is fairly accurate. Things are looking up. As we approach the cloud bank, we see that it is actually hovering over hard land. Or maybe soft tundra. Either way, this sight is welcome as all get out.

The coastline is awful slow in coming up, and it makes us wonder if our headwind is greater than forecast. That could be disheartening.

Using the compass and the contrails, I keep navigating. Epps, uncharacteristically, is still pensive. Or maybe he really is asleep.

As we finally come up on the Labrador coast, we pick up a radio navigation beacon from Goose Bay. The fuel gauge needle on the right tank is starting to bounce off the "E". The radio beacon tells us that we're off course. Pat calculates we are 50 miles north of where we should be and we have 160 miles to Goose Bay. Fortunately, the off-course difference is only two minutes flying time. That's two minutes we gave away to have the easy navigation using contrail shadows. If we make it, it was a good trade-off.

Pat does some more calculations, "We're good for Goose."

"What do you mean?"

"We'll land at Goose with plenty of juice."

"That's pretty poetic, Klondike."

He doesn't answer so I'm not sure he caught it. His brain is still running figures. But this is simple math. At the shoreline, we will have 150 miles to Goose; call it a short hour. The motor is drinking twelve gallons an hour. The Reserve and the left wing tanks are dry, and the right tank is now bumpin' on "Empty."

There are two ways to handle the next hour. One is to start a long, gradual descent at 90 miles out. Throttling back will reduce the fuel consumption and increase the speed, and maybe reduce the flight time by a few minutes. That could be a lifetime. The other option is to remain at 9,000 feet until we can see the airport. Then if the engine poops out, we can glide to it and make a dead stick landing. Both options have merits. I opt for maintaining altitude. My feeling is that there is a three-minute higher risk of running out of gas at 9,000 feet, but the options for picking a survivable landing spot are significantly increased. I hate to say it, but I think we are going to run out of fuel and plan accordingly. Fuel exhaustion at low altitude leaves precious few options.

I tell Pat, "I'm gonna stay up here all the way to the airport."

He knows the choices, "Be my guest." He likes that phrase.

Also, this is his plane and he knows the personality of the gas gauges better than anybody. Maybe this is why he's not as uptight as I am. I hope he knows something I don't know. I'm counting time, not gallons. My calculations come up with the seven-hour fuel time limit being seven minutes short of Goose. That is four minutes longer than the three minutes we'd save by starting our descent now. Said another way, I think we're at least a couple of minutes short. But if we're going to run out of gas, I still want it at 9,000 feet, not at 1,000 feet. With a dead engine descent rate of 1,000 feet per minute, that gives us nine minutes glide from our 9,000 foot altitude. That'll be almost twenty miles. Maybe that will cover our asses.

As we cross the Labrador coastline, the weather stays clear and smooth. There is a line of cloud along the shore and scattered stuff spreading across the inland lakes. The big worry — ditching in the Atlantic — is over. Man, what a relief. We know we can now survive a forced landing. The only remaining challenge is to land at Goose with a shiny, unblemished airplane.

At 30 miles out, we spot the airport. We're still at 9,000 feet. I throttle back and hold the extra altitude all the way to the landing pattern. Tower clears us to land, but I'm still ready to dead-stick it in if the engine quits. I throttle back a little more and descend within gliding distance from the field.

The motor keeps purring. And it keeps purring as we roll on the runway like we just got home from the convenience store.

The gas truck tops us off and there are nearly two gallons left in the right tank. That's seven or maybe eight minutes flying time.

"I told you we had plenty of gas. I had it all figured out. My leg. Lez go."

In an hour, we're back in the air and on our way down to Halifax, Nova Scotia; it's 630 miles away. All the distances are big up here. As we close in on the city, it's getting dark and the weather gets worse. We ask Air Traffic Control for an instrument approach. I spread out the charts and approach plates on my lap. I'm having a real problem understanding the controller's heavy French accent. It's embarrassing to admit, but I get confused in the headings and altitudes they are assigning us. But Pat is Left Seat, and he's cool as a cucumber.

"Klondike, are you catching all this? Man, I am behind. Does he have us on a right downwind leg or left downwind?"

He reaches over to the chart on my leg and points with a stubby finger. "We're right here going thisa way."

Pat follows the approach control headings obediently, bends around for the Instrument Landing System, and, in a light drizzle, paints the wheels on the wet numbers at the approach end of the runway.

It just occurred to me. Pat probably speaks fluent pigeon French and understood all the communications perfectly. Any way you slice it, *he da man*.

We catch a taxi to a small hotel in the historic part of town, and I enjoy a pair of Labatt's Blues. Epps sips a "white". We have an incredible lobster dinner and speed-walk through the historic district. Feeling invincible again, we go back to the hotel and call home. That's two calls' home in one day!

Life is good.

The morning breaks sunny and clear, so we hike up to the top of Citadel Hill. The weather is cool, fresh and breezy. From the old ramparts, there is a commanding view of the city. The river and the harbor are elegant and impressive. The harbor gives a sense of commercial enterprise. The historical buildings are comfortable with the new architecture. What a beautiful city.

After we're all pumped up on culture, we flag down a taxi and ask the driver to run us out to Peggy's Cove. It must be a 40-mile trip, but the simplicity and the beauty of the countryside make it worth it. Besides, we still have some money in the kitty.

If there is a fault with this destination, it's that the place is so picture postcard perfect that it looks like a stage set. The homes and the boathouses are all weathered wood, finished to a perfect silver-grey tint. An abandoned dinghy lies at a relaxed angle on the shore. Poppies are growing up between the deck slats. Worn nets are draped haphazardly on racks, and, of course, there are endless lobster pots stacked up and scattered about. Hell, we even have a light fog coming in off the ocean. The natural elegance of this place is unreal. It's a complete portraiture of the life, struggle and death of mankind. We do our duty with our little point-and-shoots and head back to Halifax in our taxi which has been patiently waiting for us.

Of course, Mr. Personality gets into an extended conversation with the driver. We learn where he lives, the amount of his mortgage, the impatience of his wife, Doris, his kids' grades and all the political dirt we can stand.

He then tells us about the Tidal Bore on the Salmon River in Truro, Nova Scotia.

"I bet you fellas haven't seen the Tidal Bore, have you? Well, Nova Scotia has the largest tides in the world, and twice a day it charges through tributaries all over the country. You guys gotta go over there to Truro and see it. You'll never forget it. The hills and all, over there, have a shape that catches and then amplifies the normal tides. It can reach 55 feet from low-to-high tide in about a six-hour period. People come from all over the world to see it."

We're both hooked. All the driver has to do is reel us in.

He drops us off at the airport; we throw our bags in the plane and taxi out. The weather is good, so we'll fly visually. Pat is Left Seat.

As we taxi out to the active runway, the Tower calls, "November 8176 Romeo, we do not have a Flight Plan on file for you, Over."

Pat's got the mic, "76 Romeo. We're not filing a Flight Plan. We're goin' visual. Over." I can already tell from his tone that this isn't going to be easy.

"Roger 76 Romeo. We need your destination, Over."

"76 Romeo is headed south."

"Roger, 76 Romeo. We have a form here that requires your point of destination. Over."

"Okay, This is November eight, one, seven, six Romeo. Write in the destination square, south, that's S O U T H, south. That's our destination, south."

Where all this stuff-and-nonsense comes from, I can only wonder. I really did want to see the Tidal Bore, and now we're going to have to go through one of these things.

After a long pause, the Tower calls back, "November 8176 Romeo, Cleared for takeoff."

Epps answers, "Roger."

When we're clear of their traffic area, I ask, "What the hell was that all about?"

"Hell, I don't know. They need to learn to not be so bossy."

Whatever was going on in Pat's mind had nothing to do with the Tower's attitude. I don't know to this day what brought on that little hissy fit. And I bet Pat doesn't either. But, if he wants to be a dip, I say have at it. No. How does he put it? "Be my guest."

To make things goofier, we aren't even going south. Truro is *northwest* of Halifax.

The flight is only 50 miles, and we find a small, unattended airstrip in the middle of what looks like an agricultural area. There is no aviation service, just a couple of parked planes. With no service, there is no car to borrow, so we walk out to the highway and stick out our thumbs. Within ten minutes, two guys on motorcycles zoom past, turn around, and come back to pick us up. The bikes are medium bore Japanese rice-rockets. The kids are dressed in jeans, tee shirts and no helmets. They are also dedicated throttle-blippers. VRIP! VRIP! VRIP! Maybe the machines don't idle. More likely, this is a signal of serious motorcycle aggressiveness. As a younger man, I competed in hundreds of motorcycle races. Having been one for too many years, I am quite familiar with immature motorcycle aggressor syndrome. This situation doesn't look good, and I'm ready to decline their invitation.

But faster than I can describe it, Pat's on the back of one of the bikes, and, VROOM, they're off, zooming down the road. I climb on the back of the other one and, VROOM, we're after them, zipping through gears at one per second.

This is absolutely crazy! Much more important, I'm scared shitless!

My charioteer has competent natural skills. His balance and his shift points are good. But he quickly shows that he hasn't learned the sensitivity of front wheel braking. This tells me he's new to performance machines, and it's certain that he's never ridden in competition. But it is his complete lack of common sense that scares me. To catch up with Epps we pass a heavy-laden truck, but we do it on the gravel shoulder on the right side of the roadway. This is stupid beyond description. When we do catch up, the boys are delighted. Now they want to race each other.

Epps' guy spins a wheel and zooms off in a spray of gravel and dirt. My guy, not to be outdone, follows suit. As we close in on Pat, his guy quickly turns onto an intersecting highway.

Fortunately, the road surface improves to become three lanes of nicely paved blacktop. They open up the throttles and, shoulder to shoulder, we're flying. I'd give anything to offer my lad a lesson in hard braking. He keeps hitting the rear brake while in a turn. I'm confident that it is my weight in the back of the bike that thwarts a spill.

This thrill ride is all of 20 minutes, but I would choose a dozen engine sputtering episodes over the ocean rather than take it again.

We get off the bikes and thank the kids. Pat is as dazed as I am. Of course it serves him right for being whatever he was with the Halifax tower. But I don't deserve any of it. I'm what you call collateral damage.

The boys drop us off at the bridge and VRIP, VRIP, VRIP, they're gone. This is where the Tidal Bore will come thundering through. An impressive six-foot countdown clock on the bridge abutment indicates that we have another hour and a half to wait. It's a good time to sit in the grass on the bank of the waterless riverbed. I lie back with my hands behind my head. The luscious green grass is fast becoming the highlight of this whole trip. We can smell rotting things in the soil and feel crawly things moving around in the tight web of turf. There are birds doing what birds do, and smog-producing traffic rumbling over the bridge. Tourists are starting to gather. Their babble and laughter are comforting. Even though we are still in remote Nova Scotia, we are back in a familiar social habitat. That said, for some reason we are also still aliens. Even Captain Klondike is quieted.

Ninety minutes without tension is its own form of pressure. But we gut it out. Eventually the big hand on the giant clock shows five minutes to go. In case we have to seek higher land quickly, we get up on our feet and join the group of perhaps 50 expectant spectators. The clock shows one minute to go. All eyes are looking downstream of the empty riverbed. The crowd's chatter fades into a soft murmur. We can feel the anticipation.

Then slowly, almost imperceptibly at first, comes the wall of water. Well, maybe wall is not the right word. It's more of a three-quarter inch shoe-mold. That's the little piece of wood where your wall base meets the floor. The raging river rivulet rounds the corner and glides silently up under the bridge and out of sight around the next bend. Eventually, the riverbed slowly rises to all of about three inches of water.

It is true that the depth of this "tidal surge" will continue to increase, and if we stay long enough it will reach several feet. But we're not waiting. The verb in Tidal Bore is absolutely correct, and we completely fell for it. We're outta here. Pat and I hitch a ride, in a car this time, back to the airport.

Pat flies Left Seat again and steers southwest to Portland, Maine. Most of the 360 miles is along the ocean coast. The beauty of the rugged shoreline and the hundreds of islands is compelling. My eyes are forever searching for new coves, small villages, rocky cliffs, patches of beach and tiny harbors with large marinas. There is something fascinating going on in every nook and cranny on the coast of Maine. We get a good laugh at ourselves when we catch sight of a sailboat regatta.

Pat calls it. "Hey, check that out. Maine's hosting an iceberg race."

U.S. Customs at Portland is just a formality and goes quickly. They are so nice that even Mr. Epps is nice back to them. That's a switch.

It's late when we check into the obligatory airport motel. The next morning we're back flying at 7:30 a.m. I'm driving. We're an hour in the air when, chart in hand, Pat pipes up, "Okay, this is your leg but here's the course to Clarion, Pennsylvania. I got some business there. We gonna stay all afternoon."

"Great. What kind of business?"

"They got an air show."

I know something is up. At dinner last night, Pat was not quite there, plus he drank lemonade while I enjoyed my requisite two beers. It never occurred to me to ask why. I figured he was doing penance for spelling SOUTH to the Tower in Halifax. It wasn't important enough to bring it up.

The manner in which he says, "They got an air show" says it all. It sounds an awful lot like, "Gentlemen, start your engines."

"So you want to watch the air show. Is that it?" I know the answer, but I want to hear how he's going to tell the story.

"No, I want *you* to watch the air show."

"So why do you think I want to watch an airshow in Clarion, Pennsylvania?"

Of course, he answers, "Because I'm flying in it."

I look over at him, and there it is, ear-to-ear. Epps is back.

This sort of stuff is hard to explain, but I'll give you my take on it. We've been pretty close travelers for a week now. We've made hundreds of decisions, some very big. All without conflict. So now Pat wants his day as Mister Hot Dog, Big Time, Aerobatic, Showtime, and Fearless Aviator. And, if I'm a good boy, he'll let me clean all the garbage out of the plane, wash the windshield, wipe the bugs off the wings, and be his gofer for coffee and donuts.

And, do you know what? I'm ready for it, right down to fetching coffee. I am confident of my piloting abilities. Pat taught me to roll and loop and other fundamental aerobatics. But he's still *the man* when it comes to flying. I had to learn to fly, and I learned well. Pat was born a flyer. Then he trained as an Air Force pilot, and then he worked for Boeing as a flight test engineer. I told you that story. No matter how good I get, I am always in his shadow. There is absolutely no shame in that.

As I think about it, and assuming that he doesn't screw up, tomorrow's air show could not be a better exclamation point to this adventure. And, personally, the idea of me being his gofer couldn't make me happier.

We sail across New Hampshire, Vermont, hundreds of miles of New York, and fly almost that far in Pennsylvania. According to my log book, that's 525 miles in 3.4 hours against a headwind of 28 miles per hour.

Set in the luscious green rolling hills of the Keystone State, Clarion is about 60 miles northeast of Pittsburgh. From our vantage point in the air, it looks like a fertile and productive landscape of biblical proportions.

The airport is rural and without the confusion of urban responsibilities. The paved 4,000-foot runway has plenty of grassy parking areas. We enter the landing pattern a little before noon, and I try to make my best air-show landing. You know, the one where the tires don't even chirp. They give a low moan as they gradually start rolling. Well, that doesn't happen. Instead they chirp sharply. But everybody knows that perfect landings are almost impossible after a long cross-country flight. It has to do with polar magnetic interference or something.

We're directed to taxi to the Participant's Parking Paddock. That puts us in the spotlight. I am proud to have Mr. Air Show himself with me. I shut down, and he gets out on the wing and waves to the crowd. And they all wave back. All eight of them. Well, maybe five of the eight of them wave. But still, my pride soars.

The pilot briefing is at 1:00 and the routines start at 2:00. Mr. Air Show is now doubling as Mr. Personality. I can see why it's not easy to act humble whilst caught up in celebrity of one's game of choice. And I know it's killing him that it's too hot for him to wear his old, time-worn leather flight jacket. But still this is the rarified element that energizes him to that higher stratum which few ever experience. I'm honored to be close to it.

After a hamburger and fries, I begin the janitorial duties of unloading our week's accumulation of trash from the plane. We've been moving with such determination that our housekeeping has suffered. It feels good to pick the plane clean and put everything in orderly stacks. And, yes, just in case you wondered, I clean the windshield and wipe the bugs off the wings for his Highness. I also stow all our loose items in the nearby hangar. Seven Six Romeo is now light and tight and ready to show her stuff.

While I'm sprucing up the airplane, a black and orange Piper Cub taxis up to the Participants Circle. The name "Debbie Gary" is painted on the side of the plane. The motor stops and the pilot, an attractive young woman, carefully unloads a bundle from the back seat. Her fellow traveler is still wrapped in swaddling clothes. Debbie is a face full of smiles. Written all over her is a woman with at least two great passions.

Of course, up comes Mr. E, or maybe it's Mr. S.E. Grin. He and Debbie are old buddies. She missed the pilot briefing, but Epps briefs her, and everything is just right!

Forty-five minutes later the air show begins. There are flybys of vintage aircraft and a couple of aerobatic routines before Pat starts his performance. His show is different from the others. He does his routine in one of the few four-seat private aircraft in the competition. His plane is a comfort machine designed primarily to carry clients or family to civilized destinations. Basically, Bonanza N8176R is a business aircraft with modifications that bring its structural capacity up to minimum aerobatic standards. But by competition standards, it is severely limited. It's underpowered, overweight, limited in G-force capacity, and wanting in large control surfaces. You can fly the routines, but they will lack the exact, crisp, eye-popping precision of purpose-built aerobatic airplanes. It's like racing the family Buick at a sports car event.

But, you know what? If you put the right guy in the Buick, every eye in the grandstands will watch only one car. Same thing happens here in Clarion, Pennsylvania. I am no exception. Pat Epps, in his airplane, bends and turns like a world-class dressage competitor. He is simply the master of his airplane. Everybody there knows it. And, quite properly, he does too.

The after-show dinner is a hearty spread in one of the hangars hosted by the Clarion Chamber. I eat barbeque, coleslaw, and baked beans at a folding table with an aircraft mechanic, his wife, and their six-year-old daughter. We're drinking iced tea and Cokes. This is America at its very best. I feel proud just sitting here.

Around 10 p.m., Epps and I find a motel down the road from the airport. There is another show tomorrow at 2:00 p.m. After that, we're going to fly to North Georgia and drop Pat off to meet his family at their cabin. It's on Lake Burton, a beautiful blue lake up in the Appalachian Mountains.

Breakfast is in the hangar, and we're off right after the afternoon routine. Epps flies the 500-mile leg to the 1,600-foot grass strip near the lake house. This is very close to the minimum certified distance needed for both taking off and landing the Bonanza. Pat knows the strip, so he wants to make the landing.

It's dusk when we start our search for the field. The sunlight from the west is just grazing the hilltops. The valleys are dark, and the lights of homes are blinking on in the villages below. There is no time to waste. Pat finds the strip and makes a low pass to both alert the residents and to check out the field for deer, broken cars, pickups and airplanes. The runway's clear. The grass clearing is dead ahead before I can see it. When the treetops pass only inches below the wheels, Pat cuts the power completely and lets the plane fall 50 feet before catching it with his unique flair. It touches down firmly. He's hard on the brakes. When we stop, we're only 50 or 60 feet from the end of the grassy area. From there, the terrain falls and disappears into darkness. The turf has not been mowed recently, so the drag from the 18 inch weeds helps the landing process nicely. On the other hand, that same drag is not good for takeoffs. In fact… well, you see the picture.

We shut the engine down, and the folks who live in the cabin next to the field come out to greet Pat enthusiastically. I have only the dimmest recollection of meeting them. My mind is piecing together a successful take-off program. Pat's in a hurry for me to get going. He yanks his gear out of the plane and throws it in a careless heap on the ground.

He's also in an order-barking mood. "Make halfway between a short field and a soft field takeoff. Start with the tail as close as you can get to those trees over there. Hold the brakes until full power. Release the brakes and hold the nose wheel off not more than a foot. Try 15 degrees of flaps. Good luck."

"Thanks Mom. See ya later." What else did he think I was going to do? Pull a Jet Assist Takeoff bottle out of my back pocket? He's right about holding the nose wheel up. It needs only to clear the grass. If it's too high, the wings won't get full lift and you may take off in a stall configuration. Not good.

But I have to tell you, normal night take offs are fun. The air is cool, there's seldom turbulence and the lack of visible distractions make the transition into a black sky wonderful.

Still, this one doesn't feel at all normal.

I taxi to the trees but it's too dark to get as close as I'd like. Without light, I cannot judge the distance of the wingtips to the trees. I have to give away maybe ten feet. That could make a difference at the other end of this takeoff.

I open the cowl flaps, hold the wing flap lever down until the indicator needle hits 15 degrees and firewall the throttle to build up my RPMs. I then take my feet off the brake pedals, lift the nose with back pressure, and start rolling. Right away, I get a bad feeling. Because of the weeds pulling on the main gear, this acceleration isn't close to what it's supposed to be. I'm using up real-estate, and the airspeed needle hasn't budged off zero. By holding the nose wheel up, the landing light only makes a light glow in the air above the field. It contributes almost nothing to forward visibility. From this corner of the field, the runway feels like about a football field length plus the end zones. At the 50-yard line, the airspeed is only 35 miles per hour. I need 75 to rotate. It's decision time, and things are not looking good. Hesitation is lethal. This is the one-byte moment. Either it's a one or it's a zero. There's no in-between.

I blinked and just overshot zero. The answer is made for me: make this airplane fly. Don't blink again. Slow down and feel like a wing, or better yet, feel like the air flow over the wing. Right now there are no more decisions to make. Just feel like an airplane that wants to fly. The determination of the nose wheel elevation is all in the elevator control. Don't choke the control wheel. Use a light touch, but be ready to grab a handful if everything goes to hell in a hand basket. Remember what Epps used to say about letting the horse have its head. This take off is now all about feel, not numbers. The numbers, in this case, are simply not going to work.

Although it was just on the edge of dark when we flew in, I saw the land falling away at the end of the runway. That image now comes back into my mind's eye.

The airspeed indicator inches up to 50. We still ain't flying. The end of the barely visible tall grass gets closer. At 65 mph, I get to the end of the runway. Now it's fly or die. I hold the nose level. Rotating the nose up on the edge of a stall is a no-no. Maybe someone more skilled than I can milk a plane up at stall speed. For me, we're either going fly or not. But we are definitely **not** going to stall on takeoff. Then, Whoosh! The ground falls away from under me. The rumble of the wheels on turf stops. This is like an aircraft carrier take off without a catapult. I immediately hit the gear-up lever and let off a little backpressure to get the plane as flat as possible to pick up airspeed. The plane sinks a little into the darkness. Actually, I can't see if it's a little or a lot. The landing light illuminates nothing. This is good. If trees come into view, I'm toast. I'm buying airspeed at the expense of a precious few feet of altitude. But once rid of the grass drag and the wheels tucked in, the Bonanza finally catches her breath and starts acting like the lady that she is.

When it feels like she is actually flying, I slowly retract the flaps and start buying a little altitude a foot at a time. Remember what Pat said a long time ago, "Flying is all about airspeed." It's dark as pitch in the valley, but still there are no trees in the landing light's bright cone. At 85 mph, the airspeed starts taking over, the plane takes a deep breath, and then it proceeds to climb almost effortlessly into the cool, dark night sky. The rate of climb indicator eases up to 600 feet per minute.

I'm on my way.

A week later I find out that Epps had walked down the field to make sure that I made it over the edge. I didn't think about looking for him. My mind was otherwise occupied. A tight, night takeoff has its hazards, but we both knew it could be done. That said, the tolerances were close by any standard. It was probably worth his little hike.

Once free of Mother Earth, and without the weight of Epps, his gear and a lot of fuel, the plane has a new spirit. We climb easily to 7,500 feet. It's relaxing to level off. I ease back the revs, close the cowl flaps and lean the engine out until the cylinder temp comes up, but she's just loafing along. To make it last, I throttle back to 50 percent power. It's quieter now. There is something very comforting beginning to happen. I'm in no hurry.

It's a melting feeling.

Initially my guess might be that it has to do with being alone; alone for the first time in a week. Sorry Epps, but I know damn well you feel the same way. Alone but not lonely is one of the great pleasures of life. I'm up here a mile high on a starry night in the troposphere where there are no pressures, ambitions, worries or anxieties. I feel no dangers or threats. There is only peace. And even though it is still a rather noisy airplane, to my ears it is also dead quiet. I won't hear the motor any more unless the sound changes.

People who think of themselves as spiritual might call all this being "in harmony with the world." I don't know. But to me moments like this are so rare that it's like a not-yet invented narcotic. My senses are razor-sharp. The night lights — both heavenly and earthly — are bright and microscopically focused. My heart stopped beating twenty minutes ago, and I don't need to breathe anymore. I am a floating force soaring somewhere between the cosmos and the carnal, but with allegiance to neither. It's not suspended animation. I am totally engaged with life. Except I'm observing it, not living it. I'm outside of myself looking in. I'm one of you guys up there. I see myself down here, sitting comfortably in the soft glow of the instrument panel. But at the same time I am sitting here looking out, wholly absorbing the night world. You might think I can't do both — that doing so is a conflict. That doesn't bother me a bit. Nothing does, least of all any philosophical inconsistency.

The flight is too short. If truth be told, it was way shorter than the forever I was hoping for.

Ten miles out from PDK, I radio the tower, and I'm back in the man-made system. There is no shock wave. I have absolutely no problem returning to the real world. Actually, I welcome it. Maybe it's like how you're supposed to feel after a religious experience or a frontal lobotomy. I don't know.

Once again, I think we can agree that rolling the Pole, by itself, was an event of limited consequence. Sure, it had never been done before, but the same is true of a million other things. As with so many events in life, the value of the experience is measured in the process, as opposed to the accomplishment. This is the case for work, marriages, sports, education, sex, raising a family and motorcycle racing. As Cunard Steamship Lines used to say in its advertisements, *getting there is half the fun.*

Then there is also the Butterfly Effect — a small cyclonic action that can grow in a disproportionate dimension. It can compound itself by influencing other subtle outside forces. It can be an almost mystical catalyst that releases hidden or suppressed forces. Or it can be the small ignitor-burst to an atomic detonation.

Pat and I still don't know it yet, but whatever it was that changed in us this week will bring us back to the Arctic again. Maybe it's having overcome what Jack London called, "the fear of the Arctic." Or maybe it is having acquired an appetite for stretching the envelope. Whatever it is, without knowing it, in the future we will both accede to the power of an undefined compulsion.

EPILOGUE

NEXT YEAR, 1981, this same Arctic wind will blow us right back to the Greenland icecap. It will be the first of seven expeditions over an eleven-year period. This will result in the recovery of Glacier Girl, the last Lockheed P-38 Lightning of the Lost Squadron to crash land on that frozen glacier in 1942.

But that's another book. You gotta stay tuned up there.

CPSIA information can be obtained
at www.ICGtesting.com
Printed in the USA
LVOW12*2045220517

535460LV00001BA/4/P